D1564143

THE UNIVERSE AND OUR PLACE IN IT

THE SUN
AND THE ORIGINS
OF THE SOLAR
SYSTEM

Edited by
Nicholas Faulkner and Erik Gregersen

Britannica
Educational Publishing

IN ASSOCIATION WITH

ROSEN
EDUCATIONAL SERVICES

Published in 2019 by Britannica Educational Publishing (a trademark of Encyclopædia Britannica, Inc.) in association with The Rosen Publishing Group, Inc.
29 East 21st Street, New York, NY 10010

Distributed exclusively by Rosen Publishing.
To see additional Britannica Educational Publishing titles, go to rosenpublishing.com.

Britannica Educational Publishing
J.E. Luebering: Executive Director, Core Editorial
Andrea R. Field: Managing Editor, Compton's by Britannica

Rosen Publishing
Nicholas Faulkner: Editor
Brian Garvey: Series Designer / Book Layout
Cindy Reiman: Photography Manager

Library of Congress Cataloging-in-Publication Data

Names: Faulkner, Nicholas, editor. | Gregersen, Erik, editor.
Title: The sun and the origins of the solar system / edited by Nicholas Faulkner and Erik Gregersen.
Description: New York : Britannica Educational Publishing, in Association with Rosen Educational Services, 2019 | Series: The universe and our place in it | Audience: Grades 7-12. | Includes bibliographical references and index.
Identifiers: LCCN 2018016349| ISBN 9781508106050 (library bound) | ISBN 9781508106043 (pbk.)
Subjects: LCSH: Sun—Juvenile literature. | Solar system—Origin—Juvenile literature.
Classification: LCC QB521.5 .S8647 2018 | DDC 523.7—dc23
LC record available at https://lccn.loc.gov/2018016349

Manufactured in the United States of America

Photo credits: Cover (top), p. 1 Carlos Fernandez/Moment/Getty Images; cover (bottom) tsuneomp/Shutterstock.com; back cover © iStockphoto.com/lvcandy; p. 7 Juergen Faelchle/Shutterstock.com; p. 11 Larry Brownstein/Getty Images; pp. 12, 14 © Photos.com/Thinkstock; p. 13 © Photos.com/Jupiterimages; p. 16 NASA; pp. 18, 37, 57, 62 SOHO (ESA & NASA); pp. 26, 32-33, 55, 70-71 Encyclopædia Britannica, Inc.; p. 29 Courtesy of Big Bear Solar Observatory, California Institute of Technology; pp. 34-35 Hinode JAXA/NASA; p. 39 NASA/GSFC/SDO/AIA; p. 41 G.L. Slater and G.A. Linford; S.L. Freeland; the Yohkoh Project; p. 43 Werner Heil/NASA; p. 47 TRACE Project/NASA; p. 50 The Royal Swedish Academy of Sciences/The Institute for Solar Physics; pp. 64-65 NASA/Johnson Space Center/Earth Sciences and Image Analysis Laboratory; pp. 78-79 NASA/GSFC; p. 81 NASA/Lunar and Planetary Institute; p. 83 NASA/JPL/Caltech; pp. 94-95 NASA/JPL; pp. 106-107 NASA/JPL/Space Science Institute; pp. 112-113 Stocktrek Images/Getty Images; interior pages background (blue triangles) DiamondGraphics/Shutterstock.com.

CONTENTS

Introduction 6

CHAPTER 1

Understanding the Sun 10

The Sun By the Numbers 19

The Internal Structure of the Sun 22

The Sun's Evolution 25

The Sun's Atmosphere 27

*Helioseismology: Mapping the Sun's
Internal Structure* 28

The Sun's Chromosphere and Corona 35

The Solar Wind 41

CHAPTER 2

Types of Solar Activity 46

Solar Prominences 56

Solar Flares 59

The Sun's Effects on Earth 64

The Science of Earth's Auroras 66

CHAPTER 3

Our Solar System 70

The Composition of the Solar System 72

Discovery of the Kuiper Belt. 74

Orbits in the Solar System 77

The Nature of Planets and Their Moons 79

Asteroids and Comets 82

The Interplanetary Medium 85

CHAPTER 4

Our Solar System's Origin 89

Early Theories on the Origin of the Solar System 90

Developments of the Twentieth Century. 92

Modern Theories 93

Formation of the Solar Nebula 94

The Inner and Outer Planets 96

Later Stages of Planetary Accretion 100

Planets of Other Stars. 100

Formation of the Outer Planets
  and Their Moons 102

The Small Bodies. 104

Ring Systems 105

The Sun's Angular Momentum Puzzle 108

Other Solar Systems 109

Planets of the Solar System 110

Conclusion. 116

Glossary 117

Bibliography 121

Index. 125

The Sun far outweighs all other components of the solar system combined. In fact, the Sun contains more than 99 percent of the mass of the entire solar system. Nevertheless, the Sun is a fairly average-sized star. From Earth it looks so much larger and brighter than other stars only because it is so much nearer to Earth than any other star. If the Sun were much farther away, it would look much like many other stars in the night sky. But if this were so, life as we know it could not exist on Earth. The Sun provides nearly all the heat, light, and other forms of energy necessary for life on Earth. In fact, the Sun provides the great majority of the energy of the solar system.

Astronomers believe that the solar system formed as a by-product of the formation of the Sun itself some 4.6 billion years ago. According to the prevailing theory, the Sun and its many satellites condensed out of the solar nebula, a huge interstellar cloud of gas and dust. The solar system began forming when the gravity of this interstellar cloud caused the cloud to start contracting and slowly spinning. This could have been caused by random fluctuations in the density of the cloud or by an external disturbance, such as the shock wave from an exploding star.

The Sun and Moon during a solar eclipse.

As the interstellar cloud squeezed inward, more and more matter became packed into the center, which became the protosun (the material that later developed into the Sun). The contraction caused the cloud to spin faster and faster and to flatten into a disk. Eventually, the center of the cloud collapsed so much that it became dense enough and hot enough for nuclear reactions to begin, and the Sun was born.

Meanwhile, away from the center, the gas and dust in the spinning disk cooled. Solid grains of silicates and other minerals, the basis of rocks, condensed out of the gaseous material in the disk. Farther from the center—where temperatures were lower—ices of water, methane, ammonia, and other gases began to form. The spinning material in the disk collided and began to stick together, forming larger and larger objects. Ultimately, some of the clumped-together objects grew huge and developed into planets.

The inner planets formed mostly from chunks of silicate rock and metal, while the outer planets developed mainly from ices. Smaller chunks of matter and debris that did not get incorporated into the planets became asteroids (in the inner part of the solar nebula) and comet nuclei (in the outer part of the nebula). At some point after the matter in the nebula had condensed and clumped into objects, the intensity of the solar wind suddenly increased. This blew much of the rest of the gas and dust off into space.

This general formation process is thought not to be unique to the solar system but rather to be how stars and planets throughout the universe develop. Astronomers have detected disks of matter surrounding newly formed stars.

The future of the solar system depends on the behavior of the Sun. If current theories of stellar evolution are correct, the Sun will have much the same size and temperature for about 5 billion more years. By then, all of the hydrogen in its core will have been used up. Other nuclear reactions will begin in a shell around the core. Then the Sun will grow much brighter and larger, turning into a red giant and expanding beyond the orbit of Venus, perhaps even engulfing Earth. Much later, when all its nuclear energy sources are exhausted, the Sun will cool down, evolving into a white dwarf star. Around it will orbit the remaining planets. They will have turned into frozen chunks, orbiting their shrunken star.

CHAPTER 1

UNDERSTANDING THE SUN

Although the Sun is a rather ordinary star, it is the source of virtually all Earth's energy. It provides the heat and light that make life on Earth possible. Yet Earth receives only about half a billionth of the energy that leaves the Sun.

The telescope has been used in solar studies since 1610. The solar tower telescope was later invented for use in solar studies. Its long focal length can give very large images of the Sun. The coronagraph, another special telescope, is used to examine the Sun's outer atmosphere. The instrument blocks the direct light from the Sun's disk, allowing the much dimmer corona to be viewed.

The Italian scientist Galileo Galilei and the German mathematician Christoph Scheiner were among the first to make telescopic observations of sunspots. Scheiner's drawings in the *Rosa Ursina* are of almost modern quality, and there was little improvement in solar imaging until 1905. In the 1670s the British astronomer John Flamsteed

The sunset over Joshua Tree National Park, in California.

and the French astronomer Gian Domenico Cassini calculated the distance to the Sun. Sir Isaac Newton set forth the role of the Sun as the centre of attraction of the known planetary system.

The sunspot cycle, a huge effect, was not discovered until 1843 by Samuel Heinrich Schwabe. The German amateur astronomer was looking for a planet inside the orbit of Mercury and made careful daily drawings to track its passage across the face of the Sun. Instead he found that the number of sunspots varied with a regular period. The Swiss astronomer Rudolf Wolf confirmed Schwabe's discovery by searching through previous reports of sun-

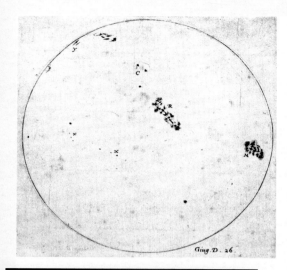

Illustration from Galileo's "History and Demonstrations Concerning Sunspots and Their Properties," or "Letters on Sunspots," 1613.

spots and established the period as 11 years. Wolf also introduced what is termed the Zurich relative sunspot number, a value equal to the sum of the spots plus 10 times the number of groups, which is still used today.

Much of the work at this time was carried out by wealthy amateurs such as Richard Christopher Carrington of Britain, who built a private observatory and discovered the differential rotation and the equatorward drift of activity during a sunspot cycle. He was the first (with another Englishman, R. Hodgson) to observe a solar flare. Photographic monitoring began in 1860, and soon spectroscopy was applied to the Sun, so elements present in the Sun and their physical state could begin to be investigated. In the early part of the 19th century, Joseph von Fraunhofer mapped the solar spectrum. At the end of the 19th century, spectroscopy during eclipses revealed the character of the atmosphere, but the million-degree coronal temperature was not established until observations of coronal spectral lines were made in 1940 by the German astrophysicist Walter Grotrian.

In 1891, while he was a senior at the Massachusetts Institute of Technology in Cambridge, Massachusetts, George Ellery Hale invented the spectroheliograph, which can be used to take pictures of the Sun in any single wavelength. After using the instrument on the great Yerkes refrac-

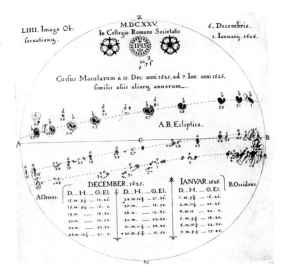

Drawings of sunspots from German mathematician Christoph Scheiner's *Rosa Ursina* (1630).

tor in Williams Bay, Wisconsin, U.S., Hale developed the Mount Wilson Observatory in California and built the first solar tower telescopes there. Prior to the construction of the Mount Wilson facility, all solar observatories were located in cloudy places, and long-term studies were not possible. Hale discovered the magnetic fields of sunspots by observing the splitting of their spectral lines into a number of components; this splitting, known as the Zeeman effect, occurs in the presence of a strong magnetic field. By continuously studying the spots for two cycles,

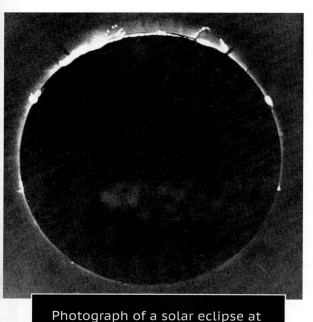

Photograph of a solar eclipse at Rivabellosa, Spain, July 18, 1860.

he discovered, with the American astronomer Seth Barnes Nicholson, the law of sunspot polarities.

Later, in 1953, the American father-and-son team of astronomers Harold and Horace Babcock, working with the same instruments, developed the magnetograph, with which the polar field was detected. In the 1930s the French astronomer Bernard Lyot introduced the coronagraph, which made possible spectral observations of the corona when the Sun is not in eclipse, and the birefringent filter, which permitted two-dimensional monochromatic images. With the Lyot filter, cinematography of the solar activity of magnetic and velocity fields became a reality. In the 1960s the American astronomer Robert Leighton modified Hale's spectroheliograph so that it could measure both velocities and magnetic fields and with it discovered solar oscillations.

After 1950, new observatories were established in areas that were less cloudy. By 1960 astronomers realized that these sites not only had to be clear but that they also had to have stable air. By locating observatories near lakes and by employing electronic imaging and vacuum telescopes, astronomers were able to make new, higher-resolution observations. In 1969 the movement began with the Aerospace Corporation Observatory (now the San Fernando Observatory) and the Big Bear Solar Observatory, both in California. Free of ground effects, these observatories achieved a new level of stable images and were soon followed by lake-sited solar observatories in India and China.

An entirely new dimension of solar studies was initiated by the space age. With one or two exceptions, all of the important spectral lines from the chromosphere and corona are in the ultraviolet, and since the photosphere is relatively weak in the ultraviolet, it is easy to disentangle the images of the upper layer from the powerful visible radiation of the photosphere. Moreover, satellites sampling the solar particles have the ability to monitor directly solar waves and particles that do not reach the ground. However, the task is not easy. Ultraviolet optics demanded special coatings and films (now charge-coupled devices) for observing. Special solar trackers were required to keep the image steady, and good telemetry was needed for the large data flow. For the corona, special coronagraphs were developed, with a series of occulting disks in front of an ultraclean lens. For X-rays, a high rate of photon detections per unit time was required to avoid early problems with pulse pile-up. The development of instruments to study the Sun also benefited the creation of satellites that explored beyond the solar system.

The U.S. Orbiting Solar Observatory series of satellites (OSO 1–8, launched from 1962 to 1975) made the first observations of X-rays and gamma rays from solar flares.

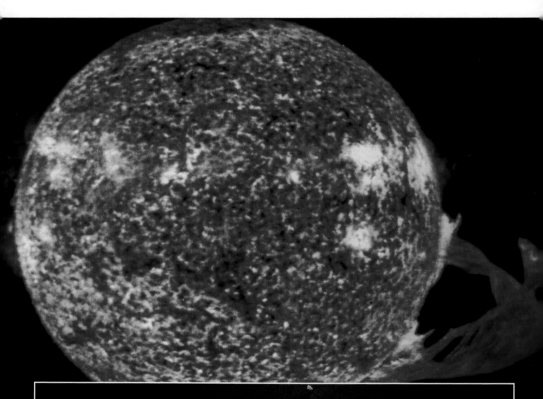

The Sun, showing a spectacular solar flare, with a base more than 591,000 km (367,000 miles) across.

They also were the first to observe gamma rays emitted from nuclear reactions in flares and to use an externally occulted coronagraph to view coronal mass ejections. A huge advance in resolution came with Skylab, a crewed U.S. space station that used leftover hardware from the Apollo project. Skylab produced the first high-resolution images in the ultraviolet lines as well as the first X-ray images of the corona. The Skylab images displayed the coronal holes for the first time, and the timing of their disk passage showed their role as a source of high-speed solar wind streams and geomagnetic disturbances.

The next important spacecraft was the U.S. Solar Maximum Mission (SMM), launched in 1980. New technological developments permitted greatly improved data, particularly on the solar-cycle dependence of the solar constant. Hard X-ray data could be obtained without saturation. In 1981 SMM's attitude control system malfunctioned, and the SMM mission was suspended until 1984 when it was repaired by the space shuttle *Challenger*.

Japan launched two very successful satellites, *Hinotori* and *Yohkoh*, in 1981 and 1991, respectively. Hinotori obtained the first measurements of a superthermal (30,000,000–40,000,000 K) cloud produced by solar flares, which is the source of the soft X-ray burst accompanying all solar flares. Yohkoh produced continuous images of the corona in soft X-rays, detected and located

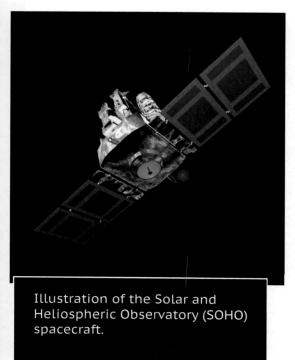

Illustration of the Solar and Heliospheric Observatory (SOHO) spacecraft.

hard X-ray bursts, and produced important soft X-ray spectra.

The European Space Agency spacecraft *Ulysses*, launched in 1990, was the first space probe to travel in a polar orbit around the Sun. It discovered that the solar wind speed does not increase continuously toward the poles but rather levels off at high latitudes at 750 kilometres (450 miles) per second.

The U.S. satellites Solar and Heliospheric Observatory (SOHO) and Transition Region and Coronal Explorer (TRACE), launched in 1995 and 1998, respectively, have produced many important results. SOHO can observe the Sun continuously, and, among its many discoveries, it has found that sunspots are shallow and that the solar wind flows outward by waves in vibrating magnetic field lines. TRACE was a powerful tool for exploring the chromosphere-corona interface and found that much of the heating in the corona takes place at its base.

The Japanese spacecraft Hinode, launched in 2006, discovered magnetic waves in the solar chromosphere that drive the solar wind. The two spacecraft of the U.S. Solar Terrestrial Relations Observatory (STEREO) mission, also launched in 2006, formed a 90° angle with the Sun in order to make stereoscopic images of it. The U.S. satellite Solar Dynamics Observatory (SDO), launched in 2010, carries three instruments that observe the Sun every 10–50 seconds to study changes that previously launched satellites were not able to observe.

THE SUN BY THE NUMBERS

The Sun is classified as a G2 V star, with G2 standing for the second hottest stars of the yellow G class—of surface temperature about 5,800 kelvins (K)—and the V representing a main sequence, or dwarf, star, the typical star for this temperature class. (G stars are so called because of the prominence of a band of atomic and molecular spectral lines that the German physicist Joseph von Fraunhofer designated G.) The Sun exists in the outer part of the Milky Way Galaxy and was formed from material that had been processed inside a supernova.

The Sun is not, as is often said, a small star. Although it falls midway between the biggest and smallest stars of its type, there are so many dwarf stars that the Sun falls in the top 5 percent of stars in the neighbourhood that immediately surrounds it.

The radius of the Sun, $R_\odot$, is 109 times that of Earth, but its distance from Earth is 215 $R_\odot$, so it subtends an angle of only 1/2° in the sky, roughly the same as that of the Moon. By comparison, Proxima Centauri, the next closest star to Earth, is 250,000 times farther away, and its relative apparent brightness is reduced by the square of that ratio, or 62 billion times. The temperature of the Sun's surface is so high that no solid or liquid can exist there; the constituent materials are predominantly gaseous atoms, with a very small number of molecules. As a result, there is no fixed surface. The surface viewed from Earth, called the photosphere, is the layer from which most of the radiation reaches us; the radiation from below is absorbed and reradiated, and the emission from overlying layers drops sharply, by about a factor of six every 200 kilometres (124 miles). The Sun is so far from Earth that this slightly fuzzy surface cannot be resolved, and so the limb (the visible edge) appears sharp.

The mass of the Sun, $M_\odot$, is 743 times the total mass of all the planets in the solar system and 330,000 times that of Earth. All the interesting planetary and interplanetary gravitational phenomena are negligible effects in comparison to the force exerted by the Sun. Under the force of gravity, the great mass of the Sun presses inward, and to keep the star from collapsing, the central pressure outward must be great enough to support its weight.

The density at the Sun's core is about 100 times that of water (roughly six times that at the centre of Earth), but the temperature is at least 15,000,000 K, so the central pressure is at least 10,000 times greater than that at the centre of Earth, which is 3,500 kilobars. The nuclei of atoms are completely stripped of their electrons, and at this high temperature they collide to produce the nuclear reactions that are responsible for generating the energy vital to life on Earth.

While the temperature of the Sun drops from 15,000,000 K at the centre to 5,800 K at the photosphere, a surprising reversal occurs above that point; the temperature drops to a minimum of 4,000 K, then begins to rise in the chromosphere, a layer about 7,000 kilometres high at a temperature of 8,000 K. During a total eclipse the chromosphere appears as a pink ring. Above the chromosphere is a dim, extended halo called the corona, which has a temperature of 1,000,000 K and reaches far past the planets. Beyond a distance of 5 $R_{\odot}$ from the Sun, the corona flows outward at a speed (near Earth) of 400 kilometres per second (km/s); this flow of charged particles is called the solar wind.

The Sun is a very stable source of energy; its radiative output, called the solar constant, is 1.366 kilowatts per square metre at Earth and varies by no more than 0.1 percent. Superposed on this stable star, however, is an interesting 11-year cycle of magnetic activity manifested by regions of transient strong magnetic fields called sunspots.

THE INTERNAL STRUCTURE OF THE SUN

The energy radiated by the Sun is produced during the conversion of hydrogen (H) atoms to helium (He). The Sun is at least 90 percent hydrogen by number of atoms, so the fuel is readily available.

The process of energy generation results from the enormous pressure and density at the centre of the Sun, which makes it possible for nuclei to overcome electrostatic repulsion. (Nuclei are positive and thus repel each other.) Once in some billions of years a given proton is close enough to another to undergo a process called inverse beta decay, in which one proton becomes a neutron and combines with the second to form a deuteron.

While this is a rare event, hydrogen atoms are so numerous that it is the main solar energy source. Subsequent encounters proceed much faster: the deuteron encounters one of the ubiquitous protons to produce helium-3 (^{3}He), and these in turn form helium-4 (^{4}He). The net result is that four hydrogen atoms are fused into one helium atom. The energy is carried off by gamma-ray photons (γ) and neutrinos, v. Because the nuclei must have enough energy to overcome the electrostatic barrier, the rate of energy production varies as the fourth power of the temperature.

The first experiment designed to detect solar neutrinos was built in the 1960s by American scientist Raymond Davis (for which he won the Nobel Prize for Physics in 2002) and carried out deep underground in the Homestake gold mine in Lead, South Dakota, U.S. The solar neutrinos in equation 1 had an energy that was too low to be detected by this experiment; however, subsequent processes produced higher energy neutrinos that Davis's experiment could detect. The number of these higher energy neutrinos observed was far smaller than would be expected from the known energy-generation rate, but experiments established that these neutrinos did in fact come from the Sun.

This discrepancy became known as the solar neutrino problem. One possible reason for the small number detected was that the presumed rates of the subordinate process are not correct. Another, more intriguing, possibility was that the neutrinos produced in the core of the Sun interact with the vast solar mass and change to a different kind of neutrino that cannot be observed. The existence of such a process would have great significance for nuclear theory, for it requires a small mass for the neutrino. In 2002 results from the Sudbury Neutrino Observatory, nearly 2,100 metres (6,800 feet) underground in the Creighton nickel mine near Sudbury, Ontario, Canada, showed that the solar neutrinos did change their type and thus that the neutrino had a small mass. These results solved the solar neutrino problem.

In addition to being carried away as neutrinos, which simply disappear into the cosmos, the energy produced in the core of the Sun takes two other forms as well. Some is released as the kinetic energy of product particles, which heats the gases in the core, while some travels outward as gamma-ray photons until they are absorbed and reradiated by the local atoms. Because the nuclei at the core are completely ionized, or stripped of their electrons, the photons are simply scattered there into a different path. The density is so high that the photons travel only a few millimetres before they are scattered.

Farther out the nuclei have electrons attached, so they can absorb and reemit the photons, but the effect is the same: the photons take a so-called random walk outward until they escape from the Sun. The distance covered in a random walk is the average distance traveled between collisions (known as the mean free path) multiplied by the square root of the number of steps, in which a step is an interval between successive collisions. As the average mean free path in the Sun is about 10 centimetres (4 inches), the photon must take 5×10^{19} steps to travel 7×10^{10} centimetres. Even at the speed of light this process takes 170,000 years, and so the light seen today was generated long ago. The final step from the Sun's surface to Earth, however, takes only eight minutes.

As photons are absorbed by the outer portion of the Sun, the temperature gradient increases and convection occurs. Great currents of hot plasma, or ionized gas, carry heat upward. These mass motions of conducting plasma in the convective zone, which constitutes approximately the outer 30 percent of the Sun, may be responsible for the sunspot cycle. The ionization of hydrogen plays an important role in the transport of energy through the Sun. Atoms are ionized at the bottom of the convective zone and are carried upward to cooler regions, where they recombine and liberate the energy of ionization. Just below the surface, radiation transport again becomes efficient, but the effects of convection are clearly visible in the photosphere.

THE SUN'S EVOLUTION

The Sun has been shining for 4.6 billion years. Considerable hydrogen has been converted to helium in the core, where the burning is most rapid. The helium remains

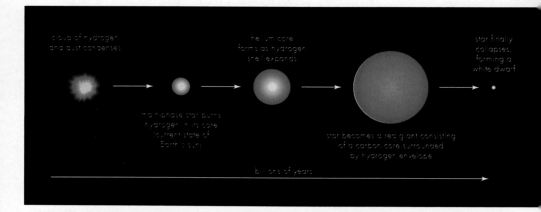

cloud of hydrogen and dust condenses

main phase star burns hydrogen in its core (current state of Earth's sun)

helium core forms as hydrogen shell expands

star becomes a red giant consisting of a carbon core surrounded by hydrogen envelope

star finally collapses, forming a white dwarf

billions of years

Illustration showing the evolution of a Sun-like star.

there, where it absorbs radiation more readily than hydrogen. This raises the central temperature and increases the brightness. Model calculations conclude that the Sun becomes 10 percent brighter every billion years; hence it must now be at least 40 percent brighter than at the time of planet formation. This would produce an increase in Earth's temperature, but no such effect appears in the fossil record. There were probably compensating thermostatic effects in the atmosphere of Earth, such as the greenhouse effect and cloudiness. The young Sun may also have been more massive, and thus more luminous, and would have lost its early mass through the solar wind. The increase in solar brightness can be expected to continue as the hydrogen in the core is depleted and the region of nuclear burning moves outward. At least as important for the future of Earth is the fact that tidal friction will slow down Earth's rotation until, in four billion years, its rotation will match that of the Moon, turning once in 30 of our present days.

The evolution of the Sun should continue on the same path as that taken by most stars. As the core hydrogen is used up, the nuclear burning will take place in a growing shell surrounding the exhausted core. The star will continue to grow brighter, and when the burning approaches the surface, the Sun will enter the red giant phase, producing an enormous shell that may extend as far as Venus or even Earth. Fortunately, unlike more massive stars that have already reached this state, the Sun will require billions of years to reach this state.

THE SUN'S ATMOSPHERE

Although there are no fires on the surface of the Sun, the photosphere seethes and roils, displaying the effects of the underlying convection. Photons flowing from below, trapped by the underlying layers, finally escape. This produces a dramatic drop in temperature and density. The temperature at the visible surface is about 5,800 K but drops to a minimum about 4,000 K at approximately 500 kilometres above the photosphere. The density, about 10^{-7} gram per cubic centimetre (g/cm^3), drops a factor of 2.7 every 150 kilometres.

HELIOSEISMOLOGY: MAPPING THE SUN'S INTERNAL STRUCTURE

The structure of a star is uniquely determined by its mass and chemical composition. Unique models are constructed by varying the assumed composition with the known mass until the observed radius, luminosity, and surface temperature are matched. The process also requires assumptions about the convective zone. Such models can now be tested by the new science known as helioseismology.

Helioseismology is analogous to geoseismology: frequencies and wavelengths of various waves at the Sun's surface are measured to map the internal structure. On Earth the waves are observed only after earthquakes, while on the Sun they are continuously excited, probably by the currents in the convective zone. While a wide range of frequencies are observed, the intensity of the oscillation patterns, or modes, peaks strongly at a mode having a period of five minutes. The surface amplitudes range from a few centimetres per second to several metres per second.

The modes where the entire Sun expands and contracts or where sound waves travel deeply through the Sun, only touching the surface in a few nodes (i.e., points of no vibration), make it possible to map the deep Sun. Modes with many nodes are, by contrast, limited to the outer regions. Every mode has a definite frequency determined by the structure of the Sun. From a compilation of thousands of mode frequencies, one can develop an independent solar

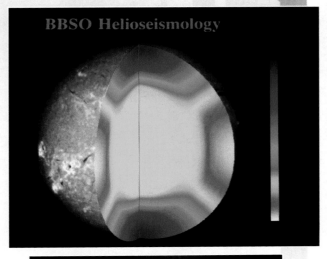

BBSO Helioseismology

The internal rotation of the Sun as a function of depth and latitude, as derived from helioseismological studies. The differential rotation is shown by the red (fast) area.

model, which reproduces the observed oscillations quite well. The frequencies of the modes vary slightly with the sunspot cycle.

As the Sun rotates, one half is moving toward us, and the other away. This produces a splitting in the frequencies of the modes (owing to the Doppler shift from the two halves of the Sun). Because the different modes reach different depths in the Sun, the rotation at different depths can be mapped.

(CONTINUED ON THE NEXT PAGE)

(CONTINUED FROM THE PREVIOUS PAGE)

The interior below the convective zone rotates as a solid body. At the surface rotation is fastest at the equator and slowest at the poles. This differential rotation is easily visible as sunspots rotate across the solar surface, and it has been known since the first telescopic studies. At the equator the sunspots rotate at a 25-day rate, and at high latitudes at a 28- or 29-day rate. The differential rotation, apparently generated by the convective zone, is thought to play an important role in the generation of the magnetic field of the Sun. Much is not understood, however, for many solar features show less differential rotation.

The solar atmosphere is actually a vacuum by most standards; the total density above any square centimetre is about 1 gram, about 1,000 times less than the comparable mass in the atmosphere of Earth. One can see through the atmosphere of Earth but not through that of the Sun because the former is shallow, and the molecules absorb only radiation that lies outside of the visible spectrum. The hot photosphere of the Sun, by contrast, contains an ion called negative hydrogen, H^-, a hydrogen nucleus with two electrons attached. The H^- ion absorbs radiation voraciously through most of the spectrum.

The photosphere is the portion of the Sun seen in ordinary light. Its image reveals two dominant features, a darkening toward the outermost regions, called limb darkening, and a fine rice-grain-like structure called granulation. The darkening occurs simply because the temperature is falling; when one looks at the edge of the Sun, one sees light from higher, cooler, and darker layers. The granules are convective cells that bring energy up from below. Each cell measures about 1,500 kilometres across. Granules have a lifetime of about 25 minutes, during which hot gas rises within them at speeds of about 300 metres per second. They then break up, either by fading out or by exploding into an expanding ring of granules.

The granules occur all over the Sun. It is believed that the explosion pattern shapes the surrounding granules in a pattern called mesogranulation, although the existence of that pattern is in dispute. A larger, undisputed pattern called supergranulation is a network of outward velocity flows, each about 30,000 kilometres across, which is probably tied to the big convective zone rather than to the relatively small granules. The flow concentrates the surface magnetic fields to the supergranulation-cell boundaries, creating a network of magnetic-field elements.

The photospheric magnetic fields extend up into the atmosphere, where the supergranular pattern dominates the conducting gas. While the temperature above the average surface areas continues to drop, it does not fall as rapidly as at the network edges, and a picture of the Sun at a wavelength absorbed somewhat above the surface shows the network edges to be bright. This occurs throughout the ultraviolet.

Fraunhofer was the first to observe the solar spectrum, finding emission in all colours with many dark lines at certain wavelengths. He assigned letters to these lines, by which some are still known, such as the D-lines of sodium, the G-band, and the K-lines of ionized calcium. But it was the German physicist Gustav R. Kirchhoff who explained the meaning of the lines, explaining that the dark lines

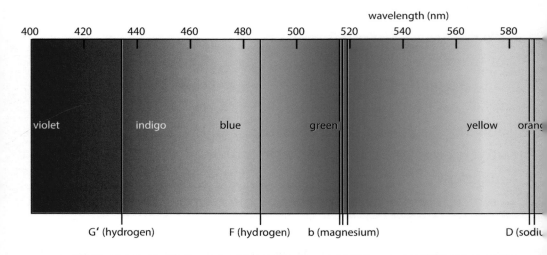

Visible solar spectrum, with prominent Fraunhofer lines.

formed in cooler upper layers, absorbing the light emerging from below. By comparing these lines with laboratory data, we can identify the elements responsible and their state of ionization and excitation.

The spectral lines seen are those expected to be common at 6,000 K, where the thermal energy of each particle is about 0.5 volt. The most abundant elements, hydrogen and helium, are difficult to excite, while atoms such as iron, sodium, and calcium have many lines easily excited at this temperature.

When Cecilia Payne, a British-born graduate student studying at Harvard College Observatory in Cambridge, Massachusetts, U.S., recognized the great abundance of hydrogen and helium in 1925, she was persuaded by her elders to mark the result as spurious; only later was the truth recognized. The strongest lines in the visible spectrum are the H- and K- (Fraunhofer's letters) lines of ionized calcium. This happens because calcium is easily ionized, and these lines

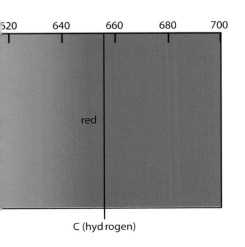

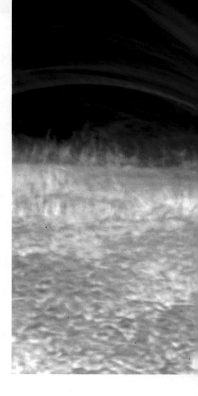

represent transitions in which energy is absorbed by ions in the ground, or lowest energy, state. In the relatively low density of the photosphere and higher up, where atoms are only illuminated from below, the electrons tend to fall to the ground state, since excitation is low. The sodium D-lines are weaker than Ca K because most of the sodium is ionized and does not absorb radiation.

The intensity of the lines is determined by both the abundance of the particular element and its state of ionization, as well as by the excitation of the atomic energy level involved in the line. By working backward one can obtain the abundance of most of the elements in the Sun. This set of abundances occurs with great regularity throughout the universe; it is found in such diverse objects as quasars, meteorites, and new stars. The Sun is roughly 90 percent hydrogen by number of atoms and 9.9 percent helium. The remaining atoms consist of heavier elements, especially carbon, nitrogen, oxygen, magnesium, silicon, and iron, making up only 0.1 percent by number.

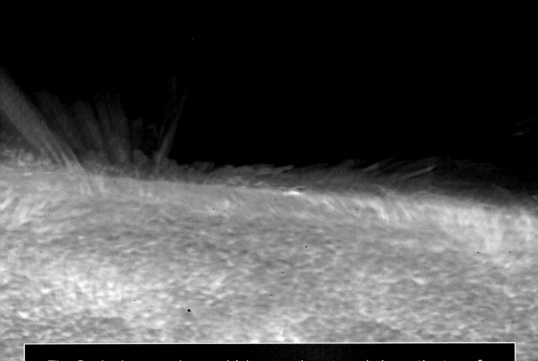

The Sun's chromosphere, which extends outward above the top of the convection cells, or granulation, of the photosphere.

THE SUN'S CHROMOSPHERE AND CORONA

The ordinary solar spectrum is produced by the photosphere; during an eclipse the brilliant photosphere is blocked out by the Moon and three objects are visible: (1) a thin, pink ring around the edge of the Sun called the chromosphere, (2) a pearly, faint halo extending a great distance, known as the corona, and (3) pink clouds of gas called prominences suspended above the surface.

The chromosphere represents the dynamic transition between the cool temperature minimum of the outer photosphere and the diffuse million-degree corona above. Because this line is so strong, it is the best means for studying the chromosphere. For this reason special monochromators are widely used to study the Sun in a narrow wavelength band. Because density decreases with height more rapidly than magnetic field strength, the magnetic field dominates the chromospheric structure, which reflects the extension of the photospheric magnetic fields. The rules for this interplay are simple: every point in the chromosphere where the magnetic field is strong and vertical is hot and hence bright, and every place where it is horizontal is dark. Supergranulation, which concentrates the magnetic field on its edges, produces a chromospheric network of bright regions of enhanced magnetic fields.

The most prominent structures in the chromosphere, especially in the limb, are the clusters of jets, or streams, of plasma called spicules. Spicules extend up to 10,000 kilometres (6,200 miles) above the surface of the Sun. Because it strongly emits the high-excitation lines of helium, the chromosphere was originally thought to be hot. But radio measurements, a particularly accurate means of measuring the temperature, show it to be only 8,000 K, somewhat hotter than the photosphere. Detailed radio maps show that hotter regions coincide with stron-

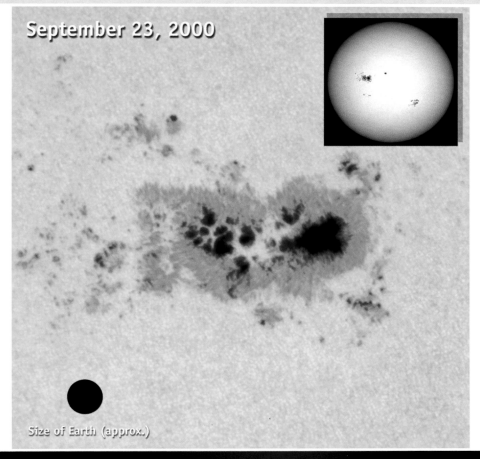

September 23, 2000

Size of Earth (approx.)

Close-up of a large sunspot group, with insets of the Earth (*bottom left*) and of the Sun (*top right*) to show relative size.

ger magnetic fields. Both hot and cold regions extend much higher than one might expect, tossed high above the surface by magnetic and convective action.

When astronomers observe the Sun from space at ultraviolet wavelengths, the chromosphere is found to emit lines formed at high temperatures, spanning the range from 10,000 to 1,000,000 K. The whole range of ionization of an atom can be found: for example, oxygen I (neutral) is found in the photosphere, oxygen II through VI (one to five electrons removed) in the chromosphere, and oxygen VII and VIII in the corona. This entire series occurs in a height range of about 5,000 kilometres (3,100 miles). An image of the corona obtained at ultraviolet wavelengths has a much more diffuse appearance as compared with lower temperature regions, suggesting that the hot material in the magnetic elements spreads outward with height to occupy the entire coronal space. Interestingly, the emission of helium, which was the original clue that the temperature increased upward, is not patchy but uniform. This occurs because the helium atoms are excited by the more diffuse and uniform X-ray emission from the hot corona.

The structure of the chromosphere changes drastically with local magnetic conditions. At the network edges, clusters of spicules project from the clumps of magnetic field lines. Around sunspots, larger field clumps called plage occur, where there are no spicules, but where the chromosphere is generally hotter and denser. In the areas of prominences the magnetic field lines are horizontal and spicules are absent.

Another important set of unknown lines revealed during an eclipse came from the corona, and so its source element was called coronium. In 1940 the source of the

A full-disk multiwavelength extreme ultraviolet image of the Sun. False colours trace different gas temperatures. Reds are cooler than the blues and greens.

lines was identified as weak magnetic dipole transitions in various highly ionized atoms such as iron X (iron with nine electrons missing), iron XIV, and calcium XV, which can exist only if the coronal temperature is about 1,000,000 K. These lines can only be emitted in a high vacuum. The strongest are from iron, which alerted investigators to its high abundance, nearly equal to that of oxygen. Later it was found that there had been errors in prior photospheric determinations.

While the corona is one million times fainter than the photosphere in visible light (about the same as the full Moon at its base and much fainter at greater heights), its high temperature makes it a powerful source of extreme ultraviolet and X-ray emission. Loops of bright material connect distant magnetic fields. There are regions of little or no corona called coronal holes. The brightest regions are the active regions surrounding sunspots. Hydrogen and helium are entirely ionized, and the other atoms are highly ionized. The ultraviolet portion of the spectrum is filled with strong spectral lines of the highly charged ions. The density at the base of the corona is about 4×10^8 atoms per cubic centimetre, 10^{13} times more tenuous than the atmosphere of Earth at its base.

Radio telescopes are particularly valuable for studying the corona because radio waves will propagate only when their frequency exceeds the so-called plasma frequency of the local medium. The plasma frequency varies according to the density of the medium, and so measurements of each wavelength tell us the temperature at the corresponding density. At higher frequencies (above 1,000 MHz) electron absorption is the main factor, and at those frequencies the temperature is measured at the corresponding absorbing density. All radio frequencies come to us from above the photosphere; this is the prime way of determining atmospheric temperatures.

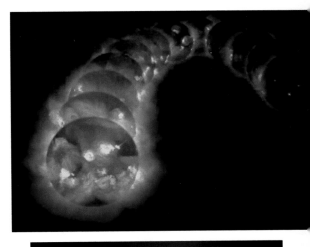

Twelve solar X-ray images of the Sun. The solar coronal brightness decreases during a solar cycle as the Sun goes from an "active" state (*left*) to a less active state (*right*).

Similarly, all of the ultraviolet and X-ray emission of the Sun comes from the chromosphere and corona, and the presence of such layers can be detected in stars by measuring their spectra at these wavelengths.

THE SOLAR WIND

The conductivity of a hot ionized plasma is extremely high, and the coronal temperature decreases only as the

27 power of the distance from the Sun. Thus, the temperature of the interplanetary medium is still more than 200,000 K near Earth. While the gravitational force of the Sun can hold the hot material near the surface, at a distance of 5R☉ the gravitational force is 25 times less, but the temperature is only 40 percent less. Therefore, a continuous outflow of particles known as the solar wind occurs, except where hindered by magnetic fields. The solar wind flows along a spiral path dictated by magnetic fields carried out from the Sun into the interplanetary medium.

There are two solar winds: a fast, uniform, and steady wind, blowing at 800 km (500 miles) per second, and a slow, gusty, and sporadic wind, with about half the speed of the fast one. The two winds originate at different places on the Sun and accelerate to terminal velocity at different distances from it. The distribution of the two solar wind sources depends on the 11-year solar activity cycle.

Where magnetic fields are strong, the coronal material cannot flow outward and becomes trapped; thus the high density and temperature above active regions is due partly to trapping and partly to heating processes, mostly solar flares. Where the magnetic field is open, the hot material escapes, and a coronal hole results. Analysis of solar wind data shows that coronal holes at the equator are associated with high-velocity streams in the solar wind, and recurrent geomagnetic storms are associated with the return of these holes.

The solar wind drags magnetic field lines out from the surface. Traveling at a speed of 500 kilometres (310 miles) per second, particles will reach the orbit of Saturn in one solar rotation—27 days—but in that time period the source on the Sun will have gone completely around. In other words, the magnetic field lines emanating from the Sun describe a spiral. It takes four days for the solar wind to arrive at Earth, having originated from a point

An illustration of the heliospheric current sheet. Its shape results from the influence of the Sun's rotating magnetic field on the plasma in the interplanetary medium.

that has rotated about 50° west (13° per day) from its original position facing Earth.

The magnetic field lines, which do not break, maintain this path, and the plasma moves along them. The solar wind flow has a continual effect on the upper atmosphere of Earth. The total mass, magnetic field, and angular momentum carried away by the solar wind is insignificant, even over the lifetime of the Sun. A higher level of activity in the past, however, might have played a role in the Sun's evolution, and stars larger than the Sun are known to lose considerable mass through such processes.

As the solar wind spreads out into an increasing volume, its density and pressure become less. Eventually the pressure of the solar wind becomes comparable to that of the interstellar medium. The termination shock, where the solar wind slows because it encounters the interstellar medium, has been measured at about 94 and 84 AU by the *Voyager 1* and *2* spacecraft, respectively. (For comparison, Neptune is the farthest planet from the Sun at a distance of 30 AU.)

Since the discovery of the nature of the corona, such low-density superhot plasmas have been identified throughout the universe: in the atmospheres of other stars, in supernova remnants, and in the outer reaches of galaxies. Low-density plasmas radiate so little that they can reach and maintain high temperatures. By detecting excess helium absorption or X-ray emission in stars like the Sun, researchers have found that coronas are quite common. Many stars have coronas far more extensive than that of the Sun.

It is speculated that the high coronal temperature results from boundary effects connected with the steeply decreasing density at the solar surface and the convective currents beneath it. Stars without convective activity do not exhibit coronas. The magnetic fields facilitate a "crack-of-the-whip" effect, in which the energy of many particles is concentrated in progressively smaller numbers of ions. The result is the production of the high temperature of the corona. The key factor is the extremely low density, which hampers heat loss. The corona is a harder vacuum than anything produced on Earth.

CHAPTER 2

TYPES OF SOLAR ACTIVITY

S olar activity follows about an 11-year cycle, in which the numbers of sunspots and other disturbances increase to a maximum and then decrease again. This activity includes sunspots, solar flares, prominences, and coronal mass ejections.

A wonderful rhythm in the ebb and flow of sunspot activity dominates the atmosphere of the Sun. Sunspots, the largest of which can be seen even without a telescope, are regions of extremely strong magnetic field found on the Sun's surface. A typical mature sunspot is seen in white light to have roughly the form of a daisy. It consists of a dark central core, the umbra, where the magnetic flux loop emerges vertically from below, surrounded by a less-dark ring of fibrils called the penumbra, where the magnetic field spreads outward horizontally.

American astronomer George Ellery Hale observed the sunspot spectrum in the early 20th century with his new solar telescope and found it similar to that of cool red

M-type stars observed with his new stellar telescope. Thus, he showed that the umbra appears dark because it is quite cool, only about 3,000 K, as compared with the 5,800 K temperature of the surrounding photosphere. The spot pressure, consisting of magnetic and gas pressure, must balance the pressure of its surroundings; hence the spot must somehow cool until the inside gas pressure is considerably lower than that of the outside.

A sunspot as viewed in ultraviolet light by the TRACE spacecraft.

Owing to the great magnetic energy present in sunspots, regions near the cool spots actually have the hottest and most intense activity. Sunspots are thought to be cooled by the suppression of their strong fields with the convective motions bringing heat from below. For this reason, there appears to be a lower limit on the size of the spots of approximately 500 kilometres (310 miles). Smaller ones are rapidly heated by radiation from the surroundings and destroyed.

Although the magnetic field suppresses convection and random motions are much lower than in the surroundings, a wide variety of organized motions occur in spots, mostly in the penumbra, where the horizontal field lines permit detectable horizontal flows. One such motion is the Evershed effect, an outward flow at a rate of one kilometre (0.6 mile) per second in the outer half of the penumbra that extends beyond the penumbra in the form of moving magnetic features. These features are elements of the magnetic field that flow outward across the area surrounding the spot. In the chromosphere above a sunspot, a reverse Evershed flow appears as material spirals into the spot; the inner half of the penumbra flows inward to the umbra.

Oscillations are observed in sunspots as well. When a section of the photosphere known as a light bridge crosses the umbra, rapid horizontal flow is seen. Although the umbral field is too strong to permit motion, rapid oscillations called umbral flashes appear in the chromosphere just above, with a 150-second period. In the chromosphere above the penumbra, so-called running waves are observed to travel radially outward with a 300-second period.

Most frequently, sunspots are seen in pairs, or in groups of pairs, of opposite polarity, which correspond to clusters of magnetic flux loops intersecting the surface of the Sun. Sunspots of opposite polarity are connected by magnetic loops that arch up into the overlying chromosphere and low corona. The coronal loops can contain dense, hot gas that can be detected by its X-ray and extreme ultraviolet radiation.

The members of a spot pair are identified by their position in the pair with respect to the rotation of the Sun; one is designated as the leading spot and the other as the following spot. In a given hemisphere (north or south), all spot pairs typically have the same polar configuration—e.g., all leading spots may have northern polarity, while all following spots have southern polarity. A new spot group generally has the proper polarity configuration for the hemisphere in which it forms; if not, it usually dies out quickly. Occasionally, regions of reversed polarity survive to grow into large, highly active spot groups. An ensemble of sunspots, the surrounding bright chromosphere, and the associated strong magnetic field regions constitute what is termed an active region. Areas of strong magnetic fields that do not coalesce into sunspots form regions called plages.

The emergence of a new spot group emphasizes the three-dimensional structure of the magnetic loop. First we see a small brightening (called an emerging flux region [EFR]) in the photosphere and a greater one in the chromosphere. Within an hour, two tiny spots of opposite polarity are seen, usually with the proper magnetic polarities for that hemisphere. The spots are connected by dark arches (arch filaments) outlining the magnetic lines of force. As the loop rises, the spots spread apart and grow, but not symmetrically. The preceding spot moves westward at about 1 kilometre per second, while the follower is more or less stationary. A number of additional small spots, or pores, appear. The preceding pores then merge into a larger spot, while the following spot often dies out. If the spots separate farther, an EFR remains behind in the centre, and more flux emerges. But large growth usually depends on more EFRs, i.e., flux loops emerging near the main spots. In every case the north and south poles balance, since there are no magnetic monopoles.

Solar activity tends to occur over the entire surface of the Sun between +/−40° latitude in a systematic way, sup-

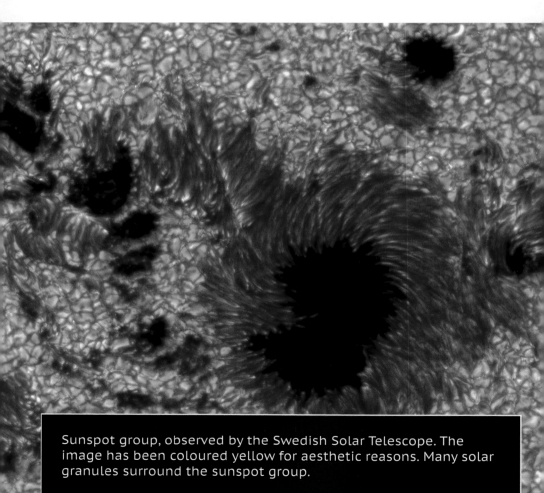

Sunspot group, observed by the Swedish Solar Telescope. The image has been coloured yellow for aesthetic reasons. Many solar granules surround the sunspot group.

porting the idea that the phenomenon is global. While there are sizable variations in the progress of the activity cycle, overall it is impressively regular, indicating a well-established order in the numbers and latitudinal positions of the spots.

At the start of a cycle, the number of groups and their size increase rapidly until a maximum in number (known as sunspot maximum) occurs after about two or three years and a maximum in spot area about one year later. The average lifetime of a medium-sized spot group is about one solar rotation, but a small emerging group may only last a day. The largest spot groups and the greatest eruptions usually occur two or three years after the maximum of the sunspot number. At maximum there might be 10 groups and 300 spots across the Sun, but a huge spot group can have 200 spots in it. The progress of the cycle may be irregular; even near the maximum the number may temporarily drop to low values.

The sunspot cycle returns to a minimum after approximately 11 years. At sunspot minimum there are at most a few small spots on the Sun, usually at low latitudes, and there may be months with no spots at all. New-cycle spots begin to emerge at higher latitudes, between 25° and 40°, with polarity opposite the previous cycle. The new-cycle spots at high latitude and old-cycle spots at low latitude may be present on the Sun at once.

The first new-cycle spots are small and last only a few days. Since the rotation period is 27 days (longer at higher latitudes), these spots usually do not return, and newer spots appear closer to the equator. For a given 11-year cycle, the magnetic polarity configuration of the spot groups is the same in a given hemisphere and is reversed in the opposite hemisphere.

The magnetic polarity configuration in each hemisphere reverses in the next cycle. Thus, new spots at high latitudes in the northern hemisphere may have positive polarity leading and negative following, while the groups from the previous cycle, at low latitude, will have the opposite orientation. As the cycle proceeds, the old spots disappear, and new-cycle spots appear in larger numbers and sizes at successively lower latitudes. The latitude distribution of spots during a given cycle occurs in a butterfly-like pattern called the butterfly diagram.

Since the magnetic polarity configuration of the sunspot groups reverses every 11 years, it returns to the same value every 22 years, and this length is considered to be the period of a complete magnetic cycle. At the beginning of each 11-year cycle, the overall solar field, as determined by the dominant field at the pole, has the same polarity as the following spots of the previous cycle. As active regions are broken apart, the magnetic flux is separated into regions of positive and negative sign. After many spots have emerged and died out in the same general area, large unipolar regions of one polarity or the other appear and move toward the Sun's corresponding pole.

During each minimum the poles are dominated by the flux of the following polarity in that hemisphere, and that is the field seen from Earth. But if all magnetic fields are balanced, how can the magnetic fields be separated into large unipolar regions that govern the polar field? No answer has been found to this question. Owing to the differential rotation of the Sun, the fields approaching the poles rotate more slowly than the sunspots, which at this point in the cycle have congregated in the rapidly rotating equatorial region. Eventually the weak fields reach the pole and reverse the dominant field there. This reverses the polarity to be taken by the leading spots of the new spot groups, thereby continuing the 22-year cycle.

While the sunspot cycle has been quite regular for some centuries, there have been sizable variations. In the period 1955–70 there were far more spots in the northern hemisphere, while in the 1990 cycle they dominated in the southern hemisphere. The two cycles that peaked in 1946 and 1957 were the largest in history. The English astronomer E. Walter Maunder found evidence for a period of low activity, pointing out that very few spots were seen between 1645 and 1715. Although sunspots had been first detected about 1600, there are few records of spot sightings during this period, which is called the Maunder minimum. Experienced observers reported the occurrence of a new spot group as a great event, mentioning that they had seen none for years.

After 1715 the spots returned. This period was associated with the coldest period of the long cold spell in Europe that extended from about 1500 to 1850 and is known as the Little Ice Age. However, cause and effect have not been proved. There is some evidence for other such low-activity periods at roughly 500-year intervals. When solar activity is high, the strong magnetic fields carried outward by the solar wind block out the high-energy galactic cosmic rays approaching Earth, and less carbon-14 is produced. Measurement of carbon-14 in dated tree rings confirms the low activity at this time. Still, the 11-year cycle was not detected until the 1840s.

The origin of the sunspot cycle is not known. Because there is no reason that a star in radiative equilibrium should produce such fields, it is reasoned that relative motions in the Sun twist and enhance magnetic flux loops. The motions in the convective zone may contribute their energy to magnetic fields, but they are too chaotic to produce the regular effects observed. The differential rotation, however, is regular, and it could wind existing field lines in a regular way; hence, most models of the solar dynamo are based on the differential rotation in some respect. The reason for the differential rotation also remains unknown.

Besides sunspots, there exist many tiny spotless dipoles called ephemeral active regions, which last less than a day

early sunspot numbers

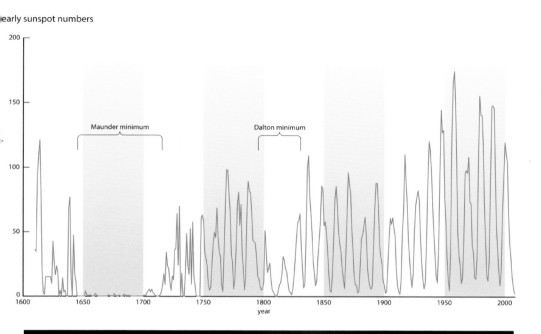

Graph of average yearly sunspot numbers showing the 11-year solar cycle.

on average and are found all over the Sun rather than just in the spot latitudes. The number of active regions emerging on the entire Sun is about two per day, while ephemeral regions occur at a rate of about 600 per day. Therefore, even though the ephemeral regions are quite small, at any one time they may constitute most of the magnetic flux erupting on the Sun. However, because they are magnetically neutral and quite small, they probably do not play a role in the cycle evolution and the global field pattern.

SOLAR PROMINENCES

Prominences are among the most beautiful of solar phenomena. They are the analogues of clouds in Earth's atmosphere, but they are supported by magnetic fields, rather than by thermal currents as clouds are. Because the plasma of ions and electrons that makes up the solar atmosphere cannot cross magnetic field lines in regions of horizontal magnetic fields, material is supported against gravity. This occurs at the boundaries between one magnetic polarity and its opposite, where the connecting field lines reverse direction. Thus, prominences are reliable indicators of sharp field transitions. (The fields are either up or down; tilted fields are unusual.)

As with the chromosphere, prominences are transparent in white light and, except during total eclipses, must be viewed in Hα. At eclipse the red Hα line lends a beautiful pink to the prominences visible at totality. The density of prominences is much lower than that of the photosphere; there are few collisions to generate radiation.

Prominences absorb radiation from below and emit it in all directions, a process called pure scattering. The visible light emitted toward Earth at the limb has been removed from the upward beam, so the prominences appear dark against the disk. But the sky is darker still, so they appear bright against the sky. The temperature of prominences is

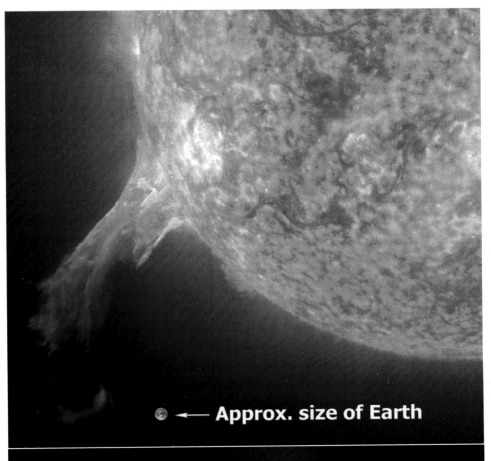

Approx. size of Earth

A close-up of an erupting solar prominence.

5,000–50,000 K. In the past, when radiative processes were not well understood, prominences seen dark against the disk were called filaments.

There are two basic types of prominences: (1) quiescent, or long-lived, and (2) transient. The former are associated with large-scale magnetic fields, marking the boundaries of unipolar magnetic regions or sunspot groups. Because the large unipolar plates are long-lived, the quiescent prominences are as well. These prominences may have varied forms—hedgerows, suspended clouds, or funnels—but they always take the form of two-dimensional suspended sheets. Stable filaments often become unstable and erupt, but they may also just fade away. Few quiescent prominences live more than a few days, but new ones may form on the magnetic boundary.

The equilibrium of the longer lived prominences is indeed curious. While one might expect them to eventually fall down, they always erupt upwards. This is because all unattached magnetic fields have a tremendous buoyancy and attempt to leave the Sun. When they do escape, they produce not only a splendid sight but also a transient shock wave in the corona called a coronal mass ejection, which can cause important geomagnetic effects.

Transient prominences are an integral part of solar activity. Sprays are the disorganized mass of material ejected by a flare. Surges are collimated streams of ejecta connected with small flares. In both cases some of the material returns to the surface. Loop prominences are the aftermath of flares. In the flare process a barrage of electrons heats the surface to millions of degrees and a hot (more than 10 million K), dense coronal cloud forms. This emits very strongly, cooling the material, which then, since there is no magnetic support, descends to the surface in elegant loops, following the magnetic lines of force.

The spectrum of prominences seen against the sky reflects their history. Quiescent prominences have no source of energy except some conduction from the corona, which is a small effect because heat cannot cross the field lines. The spectrum is similar to the chromosphere, except in the chromosphere, spicule motions produce broad lines, while the prominence lines are quite narrow until they erupt, indicating little internal motion. Surges and sprays also usually display low excitation because they are often cool material seized and ejected by magnetic forces. Loop prominences, on the other hand, are cooling from a very hot post-flare coronal condensation and have just become visible. Thus, they show high-excitation lines of ionized helium and strong ultraviolet emission, as befits a gas at 30,000 to 100,000 K.

SOLAR FLARES

The most spectacular phenomenon related to sunspot activity is the solar flare, which is an abrupt release of magnetic energy from the sunspot region. Despite the great energy involved, most flares are almost invisible in ordinary light because the energy release takes place in the transparent atmosphere, and only the photosphere, which relatively little energy reaches, can be seen in visible light.

The energy released in a great flare can reach 10^{33} ergs, which is equal to the output of the entire Sun in 0.25 second. Most of this energy is initially released in high-energy electrons and protons, and the optical emission is a secondary effect caused by the particles impacting the chromosphere.

There is a wide range of flare size, from giant events that shower Earth with particles to brightenings that are barely detectable. Flares are usually classified by their associated flux of X-rays having wavelengths between one and eight angstroms: Cn, Mn, or Xn for flux greater than 10^{-6}, 10^{-5}, and 10^{-4} watts per square metre (W/m²), respectively, where the integer n gives the flux for each power of 10. Thus, M3 corresponds to a flux of 3×10^{-5} W/m² at Earth. This index is not linear in flare energy since it measures only the peak, not the total, emission.

The energy released in the three or four biggest flares each year is equivalent to the sum of the energies produced in all the small flares. A flare can be likened to a giant natural synchrotron accelerating vast numbers of electrons and ions to energies above 10,000 electron volts (keV) and protons to more than a million electron volts (MeV). Almost all the flare energy initially goes into these high-energy particles, which subsequently heat the atmosphere or travel into interplanetary space. The electrons produce X-ray bursts and radio bursts and also heat the surface. The protons produce gamma-ray lines by collisionally exciting or splitting surface nuclei. Both electrons and protons propagate to Earth; the clouds of protons bombard Earth in big flares. Most of the energy heats the surface and produces a hot (40,000,000 K) and dense cloud of coronal gas, which is the source of the X-rays. As this cloud cools, the elegant loop prominences appear and rain down to the surface.

The kinds of particles produced by flares vary somewhat with the place of acceleration. There are not enough particles between the Sun and Earth for ionizing collisions to occur, so they preserve their original state of ionization. Particles accelerated in the corona by shock waves show a typical coronal ionization of 2,000,000 K. Particles accelerated in the flare body show a much higher ionization and remarkably high concentrations of helium-3, a rare helium isotope with only one neutron.

Because flares generally occur in strong magnetic fields, it was natural to look for magnetic changes associated with them. The Russian astronomer A.B. Severny was the first to apply the newly developed Babcock magnetograph to this task. He found that the optical flares occur along neutral lines—i.e., boundaries between regions of opposite magnetic polarity. Actually this property is dictated by the fact that flares occur above the surface, that

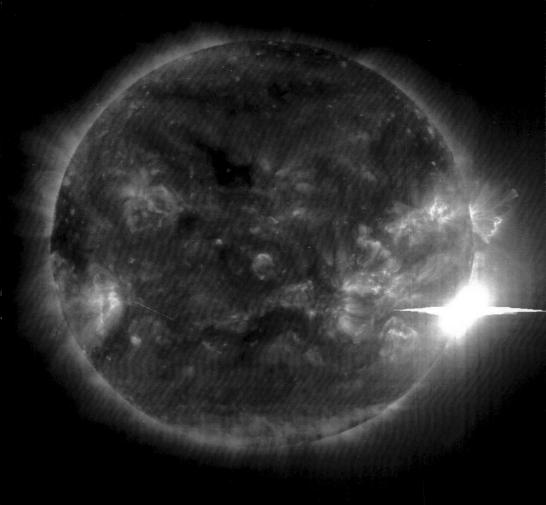

One of the strongest solar flares ever detected, in an extreme ultraviolet (false-colour) image of the Sun taken by the Solar and Heliospheric Observatory (SOHO) satellite, November 4, 2003.

the energy flows down along lines of force, and that all magnetic lines of force have two ends, leading from north to south poles.

Since the main energy release in flares is the acceleration of electrons, imaging this process shows where it takes place. While the data are sketchy, it appears that the initial energy release is above the magnetic neutral line. The electrons travel down field lines and produce bright ribbons on the surface, from which material boils up and produces the soft X-ray source, a cloud with a temperature up to 50,000,000 K. The energetic protons bombard the surface and produce a number of important nuclear reactions, which radiate gamma rays in both lines and a continuum. Among the most important lines are the positron-electron annihilation line at 0.5 MeV and the neutron-proton capture (forming a deuteron) at 2.2 MeV, as well as a number of nuclear excitation lines produced by protons incident on heavier nuclei. These lines are a powerful tool for flare analysis.

Most of the great flares occur in a small number of superactive large sunspot groups. The groups are characterized by a large cluster of spots of one magnetic polarity surrounded by the opposite polarity. Although the occurrence of flares can be predicted from the presence of such spots, researchers cannot predict when these mighty regions will emerge from below the surface, nor do they know what produces them. Those that we see form on the disk usually develop complexity by successive eruption of different flux loops. This is no accident, however; the flux loop is already complex below the surface.

THE SUN'S EFFECTS ON EARTH

Besides providing light and heat, the Sun affects Earth through its ultraviolet radiation, the steady stream of the solar wind, and the particle storms of great flares. The near-ultraviolet radiation from the Sun produces the ozone layer, which in turn shields the planet from such radiation. The other effects, which give rise to effects on Earth called space weather, vary greatly. The soft (long-wavelength) X-rays from the solar corona produce those layers of the ionosphere that make short-wave radio communication possible. When solar activity increases, the soft X-ray emission from the corona (slowly varying) and flares (impulsive) increases, producing a better reflecting layer but eventually increasing ionospheric density until radio waves are absorbed and shortwave communications are hampered. The harder (shorter wavelength) X-ray pulses from flares ionize the lowest ionospheric layer (D-layer), producing radio fade-outs.

Earth's rotating magnetic field is strong enough to block the solar wind, forming the magnetosphere, around which the solar particles and fields flow. On the side opposite to the Sun, the field lines stretch out in a structure called

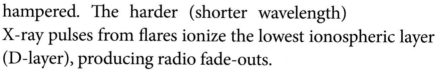

A display of aurora australis, or southern lights, manifesting itself as a glowing loop.

the magnetotail. When shocks arrive in the solar wind, a short, sharp increase in the field of Earth is produced. When the interplanetary field switches to a direction opposite Earth's field, or when big clouds of particles enter it, the magnetic fields in the magnetotail reconnect and energy is released, producing the aurora borealis (northern lights).

THE SCIENCE OF EARTH'S AURORAS

Earth's auroras are luminous phenomenon of the upper atmosphere that occurs primarily in high latitudes of both hemispheres; auroras in the Northern Hemisphere are called aurora borealis, aurora polaris, or northern lights, and in the Southern Hemisphere aurora australis, or southern lights.

Auroras are caused by the interaction of energetic particles (electrons and protons) of the solar wind with atoms of the upper atmosphere. Such interaction is confined for the most part to high latitudes in oval-shaped zones that surround Earth's magnetic poles and maintain a more or less fixed orientation with respect to the Sun. During periods of low solar activity, the auroral zones shift poleward. During periods of intense solar activity, auroras occasionally extend to the middle latitudes; for example, the aurora borealis has been seen as far south as 40° latitude in the United States. Auroral emissions typically occur at altitudes of about 100 km (60 miles); however, they may occur anywhere between 80 and 250 km (about 50 to 155 miles) above Earth's surface.

Auroras take many forms, including luminous curtains, arcs, bands, and patches. The uniform arc is the most stable form of aurora, sometimes persisting for hours without noticeable variation. However, in a great display, other forms appear, commonly undergoing dramatic variation. The lower edges of the arcs and folds are usually much more sharply defined than the upper parts. Greenish rays may cover most of the sky poleward of the magnetic zenith, ending in an arc that is usually folded and sometimes edged with a lower red border that may ripple like drapery. The display ends with a poleward retreat of the auroral forms, the rays gradually degenerating into diffuse areas of white light.

Auroras receive their energy from charged particles traveling between the Sun and Earth along bundled, ropelike magnetic fields. The particles are driven by the solar wind, captured by Earth's magnetic field, and conducted downward toward the magnetic poles. They collide with oxygen and nitrogen atoms, knocking away electrons to leave ions in excited states. These ions emit radiation at various wavelengths, creating the characteristic colours (red or greenish blue) of the aurora.

In addition to Earth, other planets in the solar system that have atmospheres and substantial magnetic fields—i.e., Jupiter, Saturn, Uranus, and Neptune—display auroral activity on a large scale.

(CONTINUED ON THE NEXT PAGE)

(CONTINUED FROM THE PREVIOUS PAGE)

Auroras also have been observed on Jupiter's moon Io, where they are produced by the interaction of Io's atmosphere with Jupiter's powerful magnetic field.

Each time a big coronal hole faces Earth, the solar wind is fast, and a geomagnetic storm occurs. This produces a 27-day pattern of storms that is especially prominent at sunspot minimum. Big flares and other eruptions produce coronal mass ejections, clouds of energetic particles that form a ring current around the magnetosphere, which produces sharp fluctuations in Earth's field, called geomagnetic storms. These phenomena disturb radio communication and create voltage surges in long-distance transmission lines and other long conductors.

Perhaps the most intriguing of all terrestrial effects are the possible effects of the Sun on the climate of Earth. The Maunder minimum coincided with the Little Ice Age, but the connection between the two is unclear. Yet most scientists believe an important tie may exist, masked by a number of other variations.

Because charged particles follow magnetic fields, corpuscular radiation is not observed from all big flares but only from those favourably situated in the Sun's western hemisphere. The solar rotation makes the lines of force from the western side of the Sun (as seen from Earth) lead back to Earth, guiding the flare particles there. These particles are mostly protons because hydrogen is the dominant constituent of the Sun. Many of the particles are trapped in a great shock front that blows out from the Sun at 1,000 kilometres (600 miles) per second. The flux of low-energy particles in big flares is so intense that it endangers the lives of astronauts outside the terrestrial magnetic field.

CHAPTER 3

OUR SOLAR SYSTEM

O ur solar system is an assemblage consisting of the Sun—which is an average star in the Milky Way Galaxy—and those bodies orbiting around it: 8 (formerly 9) planets with about 170 known

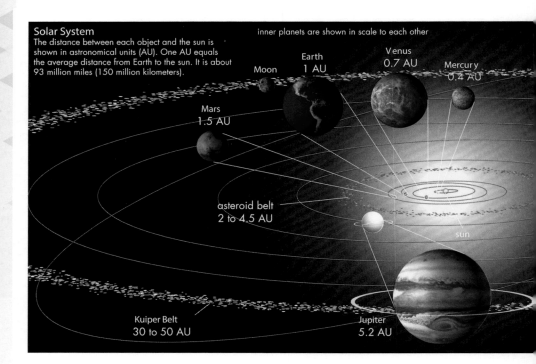

Solar System
The distance between each object and the sun is shown in astronomical units (AU). One AU equals the average distance from Earth to the sun. It is about 93 million miles (150 million kilometers).

inner planets are shown in scale to each other

Moon
Earth
1 AU

Venus
0.7 AU

Mercury
0.4 AU

Mars
1.5 AU

asteroid belt
2 to 4.5 AU

sun

Kuiper Belt
30 to 50 AU

Jupiter
5.2 AU

planetary satellites (moons); countless asteroids, some with their own satellites; comets and other icy bodies; and vast reaches of highly tenuous gas and dust known as the interplanetary medium.

The Sun, Moon, and brightest planets were visible to the naked eyes of ancient astronomers, and their observations and calculations of the movements of these bodies gave rise to the science of astronomy. Today the amount of information on the motions, properties, and compositions of the planets and smaller bodies has grown to immense proportions, and the range of observational instruments has extended far beyond the solar system to other galaxies

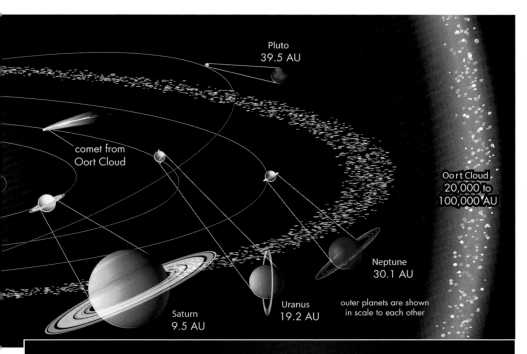

Pluto
39.5 AU

comet from
Oort Cloud

Oort Cloud
20,000 to
100,000 AU

Neptune
30.1 AU

Uranus
19.2 AU

outer planets are shown
in scale to each other

Saturn
9.5 AU

An illustration of the orbits of the planets and other bodies of the solar system.

and the edge of the known universe. Yet the solar system and its immediate outer boundary still represent the limit of our physical reach, and they remain the core of our theoretical understanding of the cosmos as well.

Earth-launched space probes and landers have gathered data on planets, moons, asteroids, and other bodies, and this data has been added to the measurements collected with telescopes and other instruments from below and above Earth's atmosphere and to the information extracted from meteorites and from Moon rocks returned by astronauts. All this information is scrutinized in attempts to understand in detail the origin and evolution of the solar system—a goal toward which astronomers continue to make great strides.

THE COMPOSITION OF THE SOLAR SYSTEM

The Sun is located at the centre of the solar system and influences the motion of all the other bodies through its gravitational force. The planets, in order of their distance outward from the Sun, are Mercury, Venus, Earth, Mars, Jupiter, Saturn, Uranus, and Neptune. Four planets—Jupiter through Neptune—have ring systems, and all but Mercury and Venus have one or more moons. Pluto had been officially listed among the planets since it was discovered in 1930 orbiting beyond Neptune, but in 1992 an icy object was discovered still farther from the Sun than Pluto. Many other such discoveries followed, including an object named Eris that appears to be at least as large as Pluto. It became apparent that Pluto was simply one of the larger members of this new group of objects, collectively known as the Kuiper belt. Accordingly, in August 2006 the International Astronomical Union (IAU), the organization charged by the scientific community with classifying astronomical objects, voted to revoke Pluto's planetary status and place it under a new classification called dwarf planet.

Any natural solar system object other than the Sun, a planet, a dwarf planet, or a moon is called a small body; these include asteroids, meteoroids, and comets. Most of the several hundred thousand asteroids, or minor planets, orbit between Mars and Jupiter in a nearly flat ring called the asteroid belt. The myriad fragments of asteroids and other small pieces of solid matter (smaller than a few tens of metres across) that populate interplanetary space are often termed meteoroids to distinguish them from the larger asteroidal bodies.

The solar system's several billion comets are found mainly in two distinct reservoirs. The more-distant one, called the Oort cloud, is a spherical shell surrounding the solar system at a distance of approximately 50,000 astronomical units (AU)—more than 1,000 times the distance of Pluto's orbit. The other reservoir, the Kuiper belt, is a

DISCOVERY OF THE KUIPER BELT

The Kuiper Belt is a flat ring of icy small bodies that revolve around the Sun beyond the orbit of the planet Neptune. It was named for the Dutch American astronomer Gerard P. Kuiper and comprises hundreds of millions of objects—presumed to be leftovers from the formation of the outer planets—whose orbits lie close to the plane of the solar system.

The Kuiper belt is thought to be the source of most of the observed short-period comets, particularly those that orbit the Sun in less than 20 years, and for the icy Centaur objects, which have orbits in the region of the giant planets. (Some of the Centaurs may represent the transition from Kuiper belt objects [KBOs] to short-period comets.) Although its existence had been assumed for decades, the Kuiper belt remained undetected until the 1990s, when the prerequisite large telescopes and sensitive light detectors became available.

The Irish astronomer Kenneth E. Edgeworth speculated in 1943 that the distribution of the solar system's small bodies was not bounded by the present distance of Pluto. Kuiper developed a stronger case in 1951. Working from an analysis of the mass distribution of bodies needed to accrete into planets during the formation of the solar system, Kuiper demonstrated that a large residual amount of small icy bodies—inactive comet nuclei—must lie beyond Neptune.

A year earlier the Dutch astronomer Jan Oort had proposed the existence of a much-more-distant spherical reservoir of icy bodies, now called the Oort cloud, from which comets are continually replenished. This distant source adequately accounted for the origin of long-period comets—those having periods greater than 200 years. Kuiper noted, however, that comets with very short periods (20 years or less), which all orbit in the same direction as all the planets around the Sun and close to the plane of the solar system, require a nearer, more-flattened source. This explanation, clearly restated in 1988 by the American astronomer Martin Duncan and coworkers, became the best argument for the existence of the Kuiper belt until its direct detection.

In 1992 American astronomer David Jewitt and graduate student Jane Luu discovered (15760) 1992 QB_1, which was considered the first KBO. The body is about 200–250 km (125–155 miles) in diameter, as estimated from its brightness. It moves in a nearly circular orbit in the plane of the planetary system at a distance from the Sun of about 44 AU (6.6 billion

(CONTINUED ON THE NEXT PAGE)

(CONTINUED FROM THE PREVIOUS PAGE)

km [4.1 billion miles]). This is outside the orbit of Pluto, which has a mean radius of 39.5 AU (5.9 billion km [3.7 billion miles]). The discovery of 1992 QB$_1$ alerted astronomers to the feasibility of detecting other KBOs, and within 20 years about 1,500 had been discovered.

On the basis of brightness estimates, the sizes of the larger known KBOs approach or exceed that of Pluto's largest moon, Charon, which has a diameter of 1,208 km (751 miles). One KBO, given the name Eris, appears to be twice that diameter—i.e., only slightly smaller than Pluto itself. Because of their location outside Neptune's orbit (mean radius 30.1 AU; 4.5 billion km [2.8 billion miles]), they are also called trans-Neptunian objects (TNOs).

thick disk-shaped zone whose main concentration extends 30–50 AU from the Sun, beyond the orbit of Neptune but including a portion of the orbit of Pluto.

Just as asteroids can be regarded as rocky debris left over from the formation of the inner planets, Pluto, its moon Charon, Eris, and the myriad other Kuiper belt objects can be seen as surviving representatives of the icy bodies that accreted to form the cores of Neptune and Uranus. As such, Pluto and Charon may also be considered to be very large comet nuclei.

The Centaur objects, a population of comet nuclei having diameters as large as 200 km (125 miles), orbit the Sun between Jupiter and Neptune, probably having been gravitationally perturbed inward from the Kuiper belt. The interplanetary medium—an exceedingly tenuous plasma (ionized gas) laced with concentrations of dust particles—extends outward from the Sun to about 123 AU.

ORBITS IN THE SOLAR SYSTEM

All the planets and dwarf planets, the rocky asteroids, and the icy bodies in the Kuiper belt move around the Sun in elliptical orbits in the same direction that the Sun rotates. This motion is termed prograde, or direct, motion. Looking down on the system from a vantage point above Earth's North Pole, an observer would find that all these orbital motions are in a counterclockwise direction. In striking contrast, the comet nuclei in the Oort cloud are in orbits having random directions, corresponding to their spherical distribution around the plane of the planets.

The shape of an object's orbit is defined in terms of its eccentricity. For a perfectly circular orbit, the eccentricity is 0; with increasing elongation of the orbit's shape, the eccentricity increases toward a value of 1, the eccentricity of a parabola. Of the eight major planets, Venus and Neptune have the most circular orbits around the Sun, with eccentricities of 0.007 and 0.009, respectively. Mercury, the closest planet, has the highest eccentricity, with 0.21; the dwarf planet Pluto, with 0.25, is even more eccentric.

Another defining attribute of an object's orbit around the Sun is its inclination, which is the angle that

An artist's rendition of a binary object in the Kuiper belt. The two objects orbit each other at the edge of the solar system.

with the plane of Earth's orbit—the ecliptic
ain, of the planets, Mercury's has the greatest
1, its orbit lying at 7° to the ecliptic; Pluto's
omparison, is much more steeply inclined, at
orbits of the small bodies generally have both
entricities and higher inclinations than those
nets. Some comets from the Oort cloud have
inclinations greater than 90°; their motion
around the Sun is thus opposite that of the
Sun's rotation, or retrograde.

THE NATURE OF PLANETS AND THEIR MOONS

The eight planets can be divided into two distinct categories on the basis of their densities (mass per unit volume). The four inner, or terrestrial, planets—Mercury, Venus, Earth, and Mars—have rocky compositions and densities greater than 3 grams per cubic cm. (Water has a density of 1 gram per cubic cm.) In contrast, the four outer planets, also called the Jovian, or giant, planets—Jupiter, Saturn, Uranus, and Neptune—are large objects with densities less than 2 grams per cubic cm; they are composed primarily of hydrogen and helium (Jupiter and Saturn) or of ice, rock, hydrogen, and helium

(Uranus and Neptune). The dwarf planet Pluto is unique—an icy, low-density body smaller than Earth's Moon, more similar to comets or to the large icy moons of the outer planets than to any of the planets themselves. Its acceptance as a member of the Kuiper belt explains these anomalies.

The relatively small inner planets have solid surfaces, lack ring systems, and have few or no moons. The atmospheres of Venus, Earth, and Mars are composed of a significant percentage of oxidized compounds such as carbon dioxide. Among the inner planets, only Earth has a strong magnetic field, which shields it from the interplanetary medium. The magnetic field traps some of the electrically charged particles of the interplanetary medium inside a region around Earth known as the magnetosphere. Heavy concentrations of these high-energy particles occur in the Van Allen belts in the inner part of the magnetosphere.

The four giant outer planets are much more massive than the terrestrial planets and have immense atmospheres composed mainly of hydrogen and helium. They have no solid surfaces, however, and their densities are so low that one of them, Saturn, would actually float in water. Each of the outer planets has a magnetic field, a ring system, and many known moons, with more likely to be discovered. Pluto has no known rings and only five known moons. Several other Kuiper belt objects and some asteroids also have moons of their own.

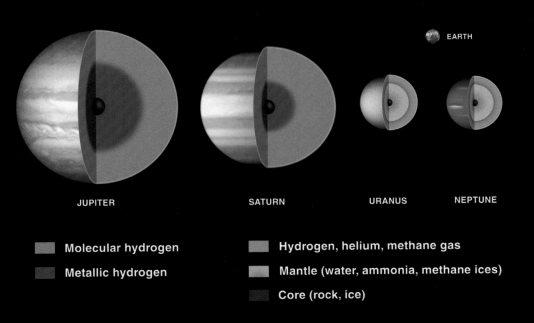

JUPITER   SATURN   URANUS   NEPTUNE

EARTH

- Molecular hydrogen
- Metallic hydrogen
- Hydrogen, helium, methane gas
- Mantle (water, ammonia, methane ices)
- Core (rock, ice)

Cross-sections of the outer planets, with an inset of Earth to show relative size.

Most of the known moons move around their respective planets in the same direction that the planets orbit the Sun. They are extremely diverse, representing a wide range of environments. Jupiter is orbited by Io, a body wracked by intense volcanism, while Saturn's largest moon, Titan—a body larger than the terrestrial planet Mercury—exhibits a primitive atmosphere denser than that of Earth. Triton moves in a retrograde orbit around Neptune—that is, opposite to the direction of the planet's orbit around the

Sun—and features plumes of material rising through its tenuous atmosphere from a surface whose temperature is only 37 kelvins (K; −393 °F, −236 °C).

ASTEROIDS AND COMETS

The asteroids and comets are remnants of the planet-building process in the inner and outer solar system, respectively. The asteroid belt is home to rocky bodies ranging in size from the largest known asteroid, Ceres (also classified by the IAU as a dwarf planet), with a diameter of roughly 940 km (585 miles), to microscopic dust particles that are dispersed throughout the belt. Some asteroids travel in paths that cross the orbit of Earth, providing opportunities for collisions with the planet.

The rare collisions of relatively large objects (those with diameters greater than about 1 km [0.6 mile]) with Earth can be devastating, as in the case of the asteroid impact that is thought to have been responsible for the massive extinction of species at the end of the Cretaceous Period 65 million years ago. More commonly, the impacting objects are much smaller, reaching Earth's surface as meteorites.

Asteroid observations from Earth, which have been confirmed by spacecraft flybys, indicate that some asteroids are mainly metal (principally iron), others are stony, and still others are rich in organic compounds, resembling the carbonaceous chondrite meteorites. The asteroids that have been visited by spacecraft are irregularly shaped objects pockmarked with craters; some of them have retained very primitive material from the early days of the solar system.

The asteroid Gaspra, which measures about 20 km (12 miles) in its longest dimension, in a composite of two images taken by the Galileo spacecraft during its flyby on October 29, 1991.

The physical characteristics of comet nuclei are fundamentally different from those of asteroids. Ices are their main constituent, predominantly frozen water, but frozen carbon dioxide, carbon monoxide, methanol, and other ices are also present. These cosmic ice balls are laced with rock dust and a rich variety of organic compounds, many of which are collected in tiny grains. Some comets may have more such "dirt" than ice.

Comets can be classified according to their orbital period, the time it takes for them to revolve around the Sun. Comets that have orbital periods greater than 200 years (and usually much greater) are called long-period comets; those that make a return appearance in less time are short-period comets. Each kind appears to have a distinct source.

The nucleus of a typical long-period comet is irregularly shaped and a few kilometres across. It can have an orbital period of millions of years, and it spends most of its life at immense distances from the Sun, as much as one-fifth of the way to the nearest star. This is the realm of the Oort cloud. The comet nuclei in this spherical shell are too distant to be visible from Earth. The presence of the cloud is presumed from the highly elliptical orbits—with eccentricities close to 1—in which the long-period comets are observed as they approach and then swing around the Sun. Their orbits can be inclined in any direction—hence the inference that the Oort cloud is spherical. In contrast, most short-period comets, particularly those with periods of 20 years or less, move in rounder, prograde orbits near the plane of the solar system. Their source is believed to be the much nearer Kuiper belt, which lies in the plane of the solar system beyond the orbit of Neptune. Comet nuclei in the Kuiper belt have been photographed from Earth with large telescopes.

As comet nuclei trace out the parts of their orbits closest to the Sun, they are warmed through solar heating and begin to shed gases and dust, which form the familiar fuzzy-looking comas and long, wispy tails. The gas dissipates into space, but the grains of silicates and organic compounds remain to orbit the Sun along paths very similar to that of the parent comet. When Earth's path around the Sun intersects one of these dust-populated orbits, a meteor shower occurs. During such an event, nighttime observers may see tens to hundreds of so-called shooting stars per hour as the dust grains burn up in the upper atmosphere of Earth. Although many random meteors can be observed nightly, they occur at a much higher rate during a meteor shower. Even on an average day, Earth's atmosphere is bombarded with more than 80 tons of dust grains, mostly asteroidal and cometary debris.

THE INTERPLANETARY MEDIUM

In addition to particles of debris, the space through which the planets travel contains protons, electrons, and ions of the abundant elements, all streaming outward from the Sun in the form of the solar wind. Occasional giant solar flares, short-lived eruptions on the Sun's surface, expel matter (along with high-energy radiation) that contributes to this interplanetary medium.

The interplanetary medium is the thinly scattered matter that exists between the planets and other bodies of the solar system, as well as the forces (e.g., magnetic and electric) that pervade this region of space. The material components of the interplanetary medium consist of neutral hydrogen, plasma gas comprising electrically charged particles from the Sun, cosmic rays, and dust particles.

Extremely small amounts of neutral (non-ionized) hydrogen have been detected throughout much of interplanetary space. At the distance of Earth's orbit from the Sun, for example, the concentration of neutral hydrogen is about one atom per 100 cubic cm (6 cubic inches). Some of the neutral hydrogen that enters the solar system from interstellar space is ionized by sunlight and by charge exchange with the plasma emanating from the Sun, called the solar wind.

The solar wind is a flow of completely ionized gas—ions (chiefly protons) and electrons—that continuously expands outward through the solar system from the Sun's corona. Its density decreases with distance from the Sun; at the distance of Earth's orbit, it has a density of about 5 particles per cubic cm (0.06 cubic inch). This outflow of plasma transports the magnetic fields of force present at the surface of the Sun radially away from it. It also is responsible for deflecting the tails of the Earth's and other planetary magnetospheres and the tails of comets away from the Sun.

Those cosmic rays detected in the vicinity of Earth comprise high-speed, high-energy atomic nuclei and electrons. Among the nuclei, the most abundant are hydrogen nuclei (protons; 90 percent) and helium nuclei (alpha particles; 9 percent). Nuclei outnumber electrons about 50 to 1. A minority of cosmic rays are produced in the Sun, especially at times of increased solar activity. The origin of those coming from outside the solar system—called galactic cosmic rays—remains to be conclusively identified, but they are thought to be produced in stellar processes such as supernova explosions.

Relatively small amounts of dust particles—often called micrometeroids—exist in the solar system, most of which appear to be orbiting the Sun in or near the plane of the solar system. Much of the dust is thought to have been produced in collisions between asteroids and in the shedding of material from comets while passing near the Sun. About 30,000 tons (27,000 metric tons) of interplanetary dust particles are estimated to enter Earth's upper atmosphere annually.

The magnetic field lines that are carried outward from the Sun by the solar wind remain attached to the Sun's surface. Because of the Sun's rotation, the lines are drawn into a spiral structure. Closely associated with the interplanetary magnetic field are electric forces that act to attract or repel charged particles.

In 2012 the space probe *Voyager 1* crossed the boundary between the interplanetary medium and the interstellar medium—a region called the heliopause. When *Voyager 1* passed through the heliopause, it became the first human-made object to reach interstellar space.

CHAPTER 4

OUR SOLAR SYSTEM'S ORIGIN

Ancient people around the globe once believed the Moon, Sun, planets, and stars were gods and goddesses, demons and angels revolving around Earth, the centre of their universe. Little did they know that Earth is a mere speck in a vast universe. It took many centuries for people to realize that Earth isn't even the centre of our solar system. A scientific approach to the origin of the solar system became possible only after the publication of Isaac Newton's laws of motion and gravitation in 1687. Even after this breakthrough, many years elapsed while scientists struggled with applications of Newton's laws to explain the apparent motions of planets, moons, comets, and asteroids. Meanwhile, the first semblance of a modern theory was proposed by the German philosopher Immanuel Kant in 1755.

EARLY THEORIES ON THE ORIGIN OF THE SOLAR SYSTEM

Kant's central idea was that the solar system began as a cloud of dispersed particles. He assumed that the mutual gravitational attractions of the particles caused them to start moving and colliding, at which point chemical forces kept them bonded together. As some of these aggregates became larger than others, they grew still more rapidly, ultimately forming the planets. But Kant did not recognize the intrinsic limitations of his approach. His model does not account for planets moving around the Sun in the same direction and in the same plane, as they are observed to do, nor does it explain the revolution of planetary satellites.

A significant step forward was made by Pierre-Simon Laplace of France some 40 years later. A brilliant mathematician, Laplace was particularly successful in the field of celestial mechanics. Besides publishing a monumental treatise on the subject, Laplace wrote a popular book on astronomy, with an appendix in which he made some suggestions about the origin of the solar system.

Laplace's model begins with the Sun already formed and rotating and its atmosphere extending beyond the distance at which the farthest planet would be created. Knowing nothing about the source of energy in stars, Laplace assumed that the Sun would start to cool as it radiated away its heat. In response to this cooling, as the pressure exerted by its gases declined, the Sun would contract. According to the law of conservation of angular momentum, the decrease in size would be accompanied by an increase in the Sun's rotational velocity. Centrifugal acceleration would push the material in the atmosphere outward, while gravitational attraction would pull it toward the central mass; when these forces just balanced, a ring of material would be left behind in the plane of the Sun's equator. This process would have continued through the formation of several concentric rings, each of which then would have coalesced to form a planet. Similarly, a planet's moons would have originated from rings produced by the forming planets.

Laplace's model led naturally to the observed result of planets revolving around the Sun in the same plane and in the same direction as the Sun rotates. Because the theory of Laplace incorporated Kant's idea of planets coalescing from dispersed material, their two approaches are often combined in a single model called the Kant-Laplace nebular hypothesis. This model for solar system formation was widely accepted for about 100 years. During this period, the apparent regularity of motions in the solar system was contradicted by the discovery of asteroids with highly eccentric orbits and moons with retrograde orbits. Another problem with the nebular hypothesis was the fact that, whereas the Sun contains 99.9 percent of the mass of the solar system, the planets (principally the four giant outer planets) carry more than 99 percent of the system's angular momentum. For the solar system to conform to this theory, either the Sun should be rotating more rapidly or the planets should be revolving around it more slowly.

DEVELOPMENTS OF THE TWENTIETH CENTURY

In the early decades of the 20th century, several scientists decided that the deficiencies of the nebular hypothesis made it no longer tenable. The Americans Thomas Chrowder Chamberlin and Forest Ray Moulton and later James Jeans and Harold Jeffreys of Great Britain developed variations on the idea that the planets were formed catastrophically —i.e., by a close encounter of the Sun with another star. The basis of this model was that material was drawn out from one or both stars when the two bodies passed at close range, and this material later coalesced to form planets. A discouraging aspect of the theory was the implication that the formation of solar systems in the Milky Way Galaxy must be extremely rare, because sufficiently close encounters between stars would occur very seldom.

The next significant development took place in the mid-20th century as scientists acquired a more-mature understanding of the processes by which stars themselves must form and of the behaviour of gases within and around stars. They realized that hot gaseous material stripped from a stellar atmosphere would simply dissipate in space; it would not condense to form planets. Hence, the basic idea that a solar system could form through stellar encounters was untenable. Furthermore, the growth in knowledge about the interstellar medium—the gas and dust distributed in the space separating the stars—indicated that large clouds of such matter exist and that stars form in these clouds. Planets must somehow be created in the process that forms the stars themselves. This awareness encouraged scientists to reconsider certain basic processes that resembled some of the earlier notions of Kant and Laplace.

MODERN THEORIES

The current approach to the origin of the solar system treats it as part of the general process of star formation. As observational information has steadily increased, the field of plausible models for this process has narrowed. This information ranges from observations of star-forming regions in giant interstellar clouds to subtle clues revealed in the existing chemical composition of the objects present in the solar system. Many scientists have contributed to the modern perspective, most notably the Canadian-born American astrophysicist Alistair G.W. Cameron.

FORMATION OF THE SOLAR NEBULA

The favoured paradigm for the origin of the solar system begins with the gravitational collapse of part of an inter-stellar cloud of gas and dust having an initial mass only

Artist's conception of a young version of the solar system depicting the dusty disks thought to be the breeding grounds of planets.

10–20 percent greater than the present mass of the Sun. This collapse could be initiated by random fluctuations of density within the cloud, one or more of which might result in the accumulation of enough material to start the process, or by an extrinsic disturbance such as the shock

wave from a supernova. The collapsing cloud region quickly becomes roughly spherical in shape. Because it is revolving around the centre of the Milky Way Galaxy, the parts more distant from the centre are moving more slowly than the nearer parts. Hence, as the cloud collapses, it starts to rotate, and, to conserve angular momentum, its speed of rotation increases as it continues to contract. With ongoing contraction, the cloud flattens, because it is easier for matter to follow the attraction of gravity perpendicular to the plane of rotation than along it, where the opposing centrifugal force is greatest. The result at this stage, as in Laplace's model, is a disk of material formed around a central condensation.

This configuration, commonly referred to as the solar nebula, resembles the shape of a typical spiral galaxy on a much reduced scale. As gas and dust collapse toward the central condensation, their potential energy is converted to kinetic energy (energy of motion), and the temperature of the material rises. Ultimately the temperature becomes great enough within the condensation for nuclear reactions to begin, thereby giving birth to the Sun.

Meanwhile, the material in the disk collides, coalesces, and gradually forms larger and larger objects, as in Kant's theory. Because most of the grains of material have nearly identical orbits, collisions between them are relatively mild, which allows the particles to stick and remain together. Thus, larger agglomerations of particles are gradually built up.

THE INNER AND OUTER PLANETS

At this stage the individual accreting objects in the disk show differences in their growth and composition that depend on their distances from the hot central mass. Close to the nascent Sun, temperatures are too high for water to condense from gaseous form to ice, but, at the distance of present-day Jupiter (approximately 5 AU) and beyond, water ice can form.

The significance of this difference is related to the availability of water to the forming planets. Because of the relative abundances in the universe of the various elements, more molecules of water can form than of any other compound. (Water, in fact, is the second most abundant molecule in the universe, after molecular hydrogen.) Consequently, objects forming in the solar nebula at temperatures at which water can condense to ice are able to acquire much more mass in the form of solid material than objects forming closer to the Sun.

Once such an accreting body achieves approximately 10 times the present mass of Earth, its gravity can attract and retain large amounts of even the lightest elements, hydrogen and helium, from the solar nebula. These are the two most abundant elements in the universe, and so planets forming in this region can become very massive indeed. Only at distances of 5 AU or more is there enough mass of material in the solar nebula to build such a planet.

This simple picture can explain the extensive differences observed between the inner and outer planets. The inner planets formed at temperatures too high to allow the abundant volatile substances—those with comparatively low freezing temperatures—such as water, carbon dioxide, and ammonia to condense to their ices. They therefore remained small rocky bodies. In contrast, the large low-density, gas-rich outer planets formed at distances beyond what astronomers have dubbed the "snow line"—i.e., the minimum radius from the Sun at which water ice could have condensed, at about 150 K (−190 °F, −120 °C). The effect of the temperature gradient in the solar nebula can be seen today in the increasing fraction of condensed volatiles in solid bodies as their distance from the Sun increases.

As the nebular gas cooled, the first solid materials to condense from a gaseous phase were grains of metal-containing silicates, the basis of rocks. This was followed, at larger distances from the Sun, by formation of the ices. In the inner solar system, Earth's Moon, with a density of 3.3 grams per cubic cm, is a satellite composed of silicate minerals. In the outer solar system are low-density moons such as Saturn's Tethys. With a density of about 1 gram per cubic cm, this object must consist mainly of water ice. At distances still farther out, the satellite densities rise again but only slightly, presumably because they incorporate denser solids, such as frozen carbon dioxide, that condense at even lower temperatures.

Despite its apparent logic, this scenario has received some strong challenges since the early 1990s. The main challenge has come from the discovery of other solar systems, many of which contain giant planets orbiting very close to their stars. These planets suggest that gas giants migrate and this may have happened early in the solar system. In one such scenario, drag from the protoplanetary disk causes Jupiter to fall inward. However, Saturn begins to form and gets locked in an orbital resonance with Jupiter. The two planets migrate outward and clear away any material that would have gone into making Mars bigger. About 500 million years after this migration, the four outer planets interact with the planetesimals of the outer disk and scatter them throughout the solar system. The final remnant of this disk becomes the Kuiper belt.

Although a number of such problems remain to be resolved, the solar nebula model of Kant and Laplace appears basically correct. Support comes from observations at infrared and radio wavelengths, which have revealed disks of matter around young stars. These observations also suggest that planets form in a remarkably short time. The collapse of an interstellar cloud into a disk should take about one million years. The thickness of this disk is determined by the gas it contains, as the solid particles that are forming rapidly settle to the disk's midplane, in times ranging from 100,000 years for 1-micrometre (0.00004-inch) particles to just 10 years for 1-cm (0.4-inch) particles. As the local density increases at the midplane, the opportunity becomes greater for the growth of particles by collision. As the particles grow, the resulting increase in their gravitational fields accelerates further growth. Calculations show that objects 10 km (6 miles) in size will form in just 1,000 years. Such objects are large enough to be called planetesimals, the building blocks of planets.

LATER STAGES OF PLANETARY ACCRETION

Continued growth by accretion leads to larger and larger objects. The energy released during accretionary impacts would be sufficient to cause vaporization and extensive melting, transforming the original primitive material that had been produced by direct condensation in the nebula. Theoretical studies of this phase of the planet-forming process suggest that several bodies the size of the Moon or

PLANETS OF OTHER STARS

The planets and other objects that circle the Sun are thought to have formed when part of an interstellar cloud of gas and dust collapsed under its own gravitational attraction and formed a disk-shaped nebula. Further compression of the disk's central region formed the Sun, while the gas and dust left behind in the midplane of the surrounding disk eventually coalesced to form ever-larger objects and, ultimately, the planets.

Understanding the solar system's origin led astronomers to wonder if other stars might also have developed planetary systems. In the glare of their parent stars, however, such small, dim objects would not be easy to detect directly in images made with telescopes from Earth's vicinity. Instead, astronomers concentrated on attempting to observe them indirectly through the gravitational effects they exert on their parent stars.

It took decades of searching to discover the first extrasolar planets. In the early 1990s, astronomers identified three planets circling a pulsar (i.e., a rapidly spinning neutron star) called PSR B1257+12. The discovery of a planet revolving around a star more like the Sun was announced in 1995. This large planet orbits surprisingly close to the star 51 Pegasi, in the constellation Pegasus.

In the first 15 years after these initial discoveries, about 200 planets around other stars were known, and in 2005 astronomers obtained the first direct infrared images of what were interpreted to be extrasolar planets. In size these objects range from a fraction of the mass of Jupiter to more than a dozen times its mass. As of 2018, there were over 3,700 confirmed exoplanets.

Astronomers have yet to develop a rigorous, generally accepted definition of planet that will successfully accommodate extrasolar planets and distinguish them from bodies that are more starlike in character (e.g., brown dwarfs).

Mars must have formed in addition to the planets found today. Collisions of these giant planetesimals—sometimes called planetary embryos—with the planets would have had dramatic effects and could have produced some of the anomalies seen today in the solar system—for example, the strangely high density of Mercury and the extremely slow and retrograde rotation of Venus. A collision of Earth and a planetary embryo about the size of Mars could have formed the Moon. Somewhat smaller impacts on Mars in the late phases of accretion may have been responsible for the present thinness of the Martian atmosphere.

Studies of isotopes formed from the decay of radioactive parent elements with short half-lives, in both lunar samples and meteorites, have demonstrated that the formation of the inner planets, including Earth, and the Moon was essentially complete within 50 million years after the interstellar cloud region collapsed. The bombardment of planetary and satellite surfaces by debris left over from the main accretionary stage continued intensively for another 600 million years, but these impacts contributed only a few percent of the mass of any given object.

FORMATION OF THE OUTER PLANETS AND THEIR MOONS

The general scheme of planet formation—the building up of larger masses by the accretion of smaller ones—occurred in the outer solar system as well. Here, however, the accretion of icy planetesimals produced objects with masses 10 times that of Earth, sufficient to cause the gravitational collapse of the surrounding gas and dust in the solar nebula. This accretion plus collapse allowed these planets to grow so large that their composition approached that of the Sun itself, with hydrogen and helium the dominant elements. Each planet started with its own "subnebula," forming a disk around a central condensation. The so-called regular satellites of the outer planets, which today have nearly circular orbits close to the equatorial planes of their respective planets and orbital motion in the same direction as the planet's rotation, formed from this disk. The irregular satellites—those having orbits with high eccentricity, high inclination, or both, and sometimes even retrograde motion—must represent objects formerly in orbit around the Sun that were gravitationally captured by their respective planets. Neptune's moon Triton and Saturn's Phoebe are prominent examples of captured moons in retrograde orbits, but every giant planet has one or more retinues of such satellites.

It is interesting that the density distribution of Jupiter's Galilean satellites, its four largest regular moons, mirrors that of the planets in the solar system at large. The two Galilean moons closest to the planet, Io and Europa, are rocky bodies, while the more-distant Ganymede and

Callisto are half ice. Models for the formation of Jupiter suggest that this giant planet was sufficiently hot during its early history that ice could not condense in the circumplanetary nebula at the present position of Io.

THE SMALL BODIES

At some point after most of the matter in the solar nebula had formed discrete objects, a sudden increase in the intensity of the solar wind apparently cleared the remaining gas and dust out of the system. Astronomers have found evidence of such strong outflows around young stars. The larger debris from the nebula remained, some of which is seen today in the form of asteroids and comets. The rapid growth of Jupiter apparently prevented the formation of a planet in the gap between Jupiter and Mars; within this area remain the thousands of objects that make up the asteroid belt, whose total mass is less than one-third the mass of the Moon. The meteorites that are recovered on Earth, the great majority of which come from these asteroids, provide important clues to the conditions and processes in the early solar nebula.

The icy comet nuclei are representative of the planetesimals that formed in the outer solar system. Most are extremely small, but the Centaur object called Chiron—originally classified as a distant asteroid but now known to show characteristics of a comet—has a diameter estimated to be about 200 km (125 miles). Other bodies of this size and much larger—e.g., Pluto and Eris—have been observed in the Kuiper belt. Most of the objects occupying the Kuiper belt apparently formed in place, but calculations show that billions of icy planetesimals were gravitationally expelled by the giant planets from their vicinity as the planets formed. These objects became the population of the Oort cloud.

RING SYSTEMS

The formation of planetary rings remains a subject of intense research, although their existence can be easily understood in terms of their position relative to the planet that they surround. Each planet has a critical distance from its centre known as its Roche limit, named for Édouard Roche, the 19th-century French mathematician who first explained this concept. The ring systems of Jupiter, Saturn, Uranus, and Neptune lie inside the Roche limits of their respective planets. Within this distance the gravitational attraction of two small bodies for each other is smaller than the difference in the attraction of the planet for each of them. Hence, the two cannot accrete to form a larger object. Moreover, because a planet's gravitational field acts to disperse the distribution of small particles in a surrounding disk, the random motions that would lead to accretion by collision are minimized.

Saturn and its spectacular rings, in a natural-colour composite of 126 images taken by the Cassini spacecraft on October 6, 2004.

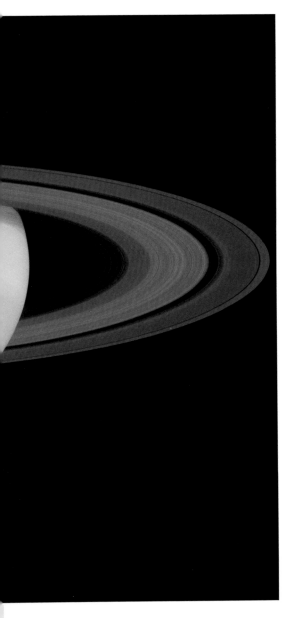

The problem challenging astronomers is in understanding how and when the material making up a planet's rings reached its present position within the Roche limit and how the rings are radially confined. These processes are likely to be very different for the different ring systems. Jupiter's rings are clearly in a steady state between production and loss, with fresh particles continuously being supplied by the planet's inner moons. For Saturn, scientists are divided between those who propose that the rings are remnants of the planet-forming process and those who believe that the rings must be relatively young—perhaps only a few hundred million years old. In either case, their source appears to be icy planetesimals that collided and fragmented into the small particles observed today.

THE SUN'S ANGULAR MOMENTUM PUZZLE

The angular momentum problem that defeated Kant and Laplace—why the planets have most of the solar system's angular momentum while the Sun has most of the mass—can now be approached in a cosmic context. All stars having masses that range from slightly above the mass of the Sun to the smallest known masses rotate more slowly than an extrapolation based on the rotation rate of stars of higher mass would predict. Accordingly, these sunlike stars show the same deficit in angular momentum as the Sun itself.

The answer to how this loss could have occurred seems to lie in the solar wind. The Sun and other stars of comparable mass have outer atmospheres that are slowly but steadily expanding into space. Stars of higher mass do not exhibit such stellar winds. The loss of angular momentum associated with this loss of mass to space is sufficient to reduce the rate of the Sun's rotation. Thus, the planets preserve the angular momentum that was in the original solar nebula, but the Sun has gradually slowed down in the 4.6 billion years since it formed.

OTHER SOLAR SYSTEMS

Astronomers long wondered if the process of planetary formation has accompanied the birth of stars other than the Sun. The discovery of extrasolar planets—planets circling other stars—helped clarify their ideas of the formation of Earth's solar system by removing the handicap of being able to study only one example. Extrasolar planets were not expected to be easy to see directly with Earth-based telescopes because such small and dim objects would usually be obscured in the glare of the stars that they orbit. Instead, efforts were made to observe them indirectly by noting the gravitational effects that they exerted on their parent stars—for example, slight wobbles produced in the parent star's motion through space or, alternately, small periodic changes in some property of the star's radiation, caused by the planet's tugging the star first toward and then away from the direction of Earth. Extrasolar planets also could be detected indirectly by measuring the change in a star's apparent brightness as the planet passed in front of (transited) the star.

After decades of searching for extrasolar planets, astronomers in the early 1990s confirmed the presence of three bodies circling a pulsar—i.e., a rapidly spinning neutron star—called PSR B1257+12. The first discovery of a planet revolving around a less-exotic, more-sunlike star took place in 1995, when the existence of a massive planet moving around the star 51 Pegasi was announced. By the end of 1996 astronomers had indirectly identified several more planets in orbit around other stars, but only in 2005 did astronomers obtain the first direct photographs of what appeared to be an extrasolar planet. Thousands of planetary systems are known.

PLANETS OF THE SOLAR SYSTEM

The idea of what exactly constitutes a planet of the solar system has been traditionally the product of historical and cultural consensus.

Ancient skygazers applied the term planet to the seven celestial bodies that were observed to move appreciably against the background of the apparently fixed stars. These included the Sun and Earth's Moon, as well as the five planets in the modern sense—Mercury, Venus, Mars, Jupiter, and Saturn—that were readily visible as celestial wanderers before the invention of the telescope.

After the idea of an Earth-centred cosmos was dispelled and more distinctions were made about the nature and movement of objects in the sky, the term planet was reserved only for those larger bodies that orbited the Sun. When the giant bodies Uranus and Neptune were discovered in 1781 and 1846, respectively, their obvious kinship with the other known planets left little question regarding their addition to the planetary ranks.

So also, at first, appeared to be the case for Pluto when, during a concerted search for a ninth planet, it was observed in 1930 as a seemingly lone object beyond the orbit of Neptune. In later decades, however, Pluto's planetary status became increasingly questioned by astronomers who noted that its tiny size, unusual orbital characteristics, and composition of ice and rock made it an anomaly among the other recognized planets. After many more Pluto-sized and smaller icy objects were found orbiting beyond Neptune beginning in the 1990s, astronomers recognized that Pluto, far from being unique in its part of the solar system, is almost undoubtedly one of the larger and nearer pieces of this debris, known collectively as the Kuiper belt, that is left over from the formation of the planets.

Broadly defined, a planet is any relatively large natural body that revolves in an orbit around the Sun or around some other star and that is not radiating energy from internal nuclear fusion reactions. In addition to the above description, some scientists impose additional constraints regarding characteristics such as size (e.g., the object should be more than about 1,000 km [600 miles] across, or a little larger than the largest known asteroid, Ceres), shape (it should be large enough to have been squeezed by its own gravity into a sphere—i.e., roughly 700 km [435 miles] across, depending on its density), or mass (it must have a mass insufficient for its core to have experienced even temporary nuclear fusion).

As the term is applied to bodies in Earth's solar system, the International Astronomical Union (IAU), which is charged by the scientific community with classifying astronomical objects, lists eight planets orbiting the Sun;

Dwarf planets Ceres, Pluto, and Eris.

in order of increasing distance, they are Mercury, Venus, Earth, Mars, Jupiter, Saturn, Uranus, and Neptune. Pluto also was listed as a planet until 2006.

In August 2006, after intense debate over the question of Pluto's planetary status, the general assembly of the IAU approved a definition for a solar system planet that excluded Pluto. At the same time, it defined a new distinct

class of objects called dwarf planets, for which Pluto qualified. Following the IAU proclamations, many scientists protested the definitions, considering them flawed and unscientific and calling for their reconsideration.

According to the 2006 IAU decision, for a celestial body to be a planet of the solar system, it must meet three conditions: it must be in orbit around the Sun, have been molded by its own gravity into a round or nearly round shape, and have "cleared the neighbourhood around its orbit," meaning that its mass must be large enough for its gravity to have removed rocky and icy debris from its orbital vicinity. Pluto failed on the third requirement because it orbits partially within, and is considered to be part of, the Kuiper belt. By contrast, Charon, by virtue of its being a moon of Pluto, is not a dwarf planet, even though its diameter is more than half that of Pluto. The ranks of dwarf planets will likely be expanded as other objects known or yet to be discovered are determined to meet the conditions of the definition.

In June 2008 the IAU created a new category, plutoids, within the dwarf planet category. Plutoids are dwarf planets that are farther from the Sun than Neptune; that is, they are the largest objects in the Kuiper belt. Two of the dwarf planets, Pluto and Eris, are plutoids; Ceres, because of its location in the asteroid belt, is not.

Of the eight currently recognized planets of the solar system, the inner four, from Mercury to Mars, are called terrestrial planets; those from Jupiter to Neptune are called giant planets or Jovian planets. Between these two main groups is a belt of numerous small bodies called asteroids. After Ceres and other larger asteroids were discovered in the early 19th century, the bodies in this class were also referred to as minor planets or planetoids, but the term asteroid is now used most widely.

The Sun can be seen as the heart of our solar system. Containing more than 99 percent of the system's mass, the Sun's gravitational pull holds the system together. Its effect on the planets and the other orbiting objects are immense.

Without the Sun's gravity, the planets would never have formed and the solar system would not exist. The Sun also drives the planets' seasons, the effects of which we're most familiar with on Earth. And the seasons influence nearly all the natural phenomena we experience.

What is amazing is that as powerful and far-reaching as the Sun is, it is not an particularly large star, even though 1.3 million Earths could fit inside it. Though as the Sun begins to lose energy in another several billion years, its life will start to come to an end. It will expand to engulf Mercury and Venus, and perhaps even Earth. It will eventually shrink to a white dwarf, bringing to an end the solar system as we know it.

The latest mission to the Sun, the NASA *Parker Solar Probe*, is designed to revolutionize our understanding of the Sun and its effects on the solar system, and perhaps other worlds. The probe will travel into the Sun's atmosphere, deeper than any other mission in history.

GLOSSARY

accretion Growth by gradual buildup.

Astronomical Unit (AU) A unit of length effectively equal to the average, or mean, distance between Earth and the Sun, defined as 149,597,870.7 km (92,955,807.3 miles).

aurora A luminous phenomenon that consists of streamers or arches of light appearing in the upper atmosphere of a planet's magnetic polar regions and is caused by the emission of light from atoms excited by electrons accelerated along the planet's magnetic field lines.

brown dwarf A celestial object that is much smaller than a normal star and has insufficient mass to sustain nuclear fusion but that is hot enough to radiate energy especially at infrared wavelengths.

convection Heat transfer, via liquid or gas, from one region to another.

Cretaceous Of, relating to, or being the last period of the Mesozoic era, characterized by continued dominance of dinosaurs, emergent dominance of angiosperms, diversification of mammals, and the extinction of many types of organisms at the close of the period.

density The mass of a unit volume of a material substance.

dipole A pair of electric charges or magnetic poles that are of equal magnitude but opposite sign or polarity, separated by a distance.

dwarf star A low-luminosity star.

friction The force that resists relative motion between two bodies in contact.

fusion The union of atomic nuclei to form heavier nuclei resulting in the release of enormous quantities of energy when certain light elements unite.

interstellar Something that is located, taking place, or traveling among the stars.

Kuiper Belt A band of small celestial bodies beyond the orbit of Neptune from which many short-period comets are believed to originate.

magnetosphere A region surrounding a planet in which charged particles are trapped and their behavior is dominated by the planet's magnetic field.

mass The property of a body that is a measure of its inertia and that is commonly taken as a measure of the amount of material it contains and causes it to have weight in a gravitational field.

nebula A mass of interstellar gas and dust.

neutrino An uncharged elementary particle that is believed to have a very small mass, that has any of three forms, and that interacts only rarely with other particles.

nova A star that brightens temporarily while ejecting a shell explosively.

nucleus The small bright body in the head of a comet.

Oort cloud A spherical shell of cometary bodies believed to surround the Sun far beyond the orbits of the outermost planets and from which some are dislodged when perturbed to fall toward the Sun.

photon A quantum of electromagnetic radiation.

planetesimal Any of numerous small celestial bodies that may have existed at an early stage of the development of the solar system.

prograde Counterclockwise motion of the planets around the Sun as seen from above the Sun's north pole.

pulsar A celestial source of pulsating electromagnetic radiation (such as radio waves) characterized by a short relatively constant interval (such as .033 second) between pulses that is held to be a rotating neutron star.

quasar The abbreviation for quasi-stellar radio source, which emits up to 100 times as much radiation as a galaxy.

retrograde Moving backward or in an order that is opposite the usual.

silicate A salt or ester derived from a silicic acid.

solar mass The mass of the Sun used as a unit for the expression of the masses of other celestial objects.

solar wind Plasma continuously ejected from the Sun's surface into and through interplanetary space.

spectroscopy The production and investigation of spectra, a continuum of colour formed when a beam of white light is dispersed.

tidal force The effect of the stretching of a body toward the center of mass of another body due to the gradient in strength of the gravitational field.

transit Event when a small astronomical body passes in front of a larger astronomical body.

velocity The rate of change of position along a straight line with respect to time.

volt A unit for measuring the force that moves an electric current.

BIBLIOGRAPHY

CHARACTERISTICS OF THE SUN, TYPES OF SOLAR ACTIVITY, AND HISTORY OF THE OBSERVATION OF THE SUN

Popular works on the Sun include Michael J. Carlowicz and Ramon E. Lopez, *Storms from the Sun: The Emerging Science of Space Weather* (2002); Leon Golub and Jay M. Pasachoff, *Nearest Star: The Surprising Science of Our Sun* (2001); Kenneth R. Lang, *The Cambridge Encyclopedia of the Sun* (2001), and *The Sun from Space*, 2nd ed. (2009). Works of a more technical nature include Peter Foukal, *Solar Astrophysics*, 2nd ed. (2004); and Markus J. Aschwanden, *Physics of the Solar Corona*, 2nd ed. (2006).

OUR SOLAR SYSTEM

Good overviews of the solar system include J. Kelly Beatty, Carolyn Collins Peterson, and Andrew Chaikin (eds.), *The New Solar System*, 4th ed. (1999); David Morrison and Tobias Owen, *The Planetary System*, 3rd ed. (2003); and Kenneth R. Lang, *The Cambridge Guide to the Solar System* (2003). David A. Rothery, *Satellites of the Outer Planets: Worlds in Their Own Right*, 2nd ed. (1999), is an excellent review of the large moons of the largest planets. William B. Hubbard, *Planetary Interiors* (1984), discusses (using much mathematics) the physics and chemistry of the interiors of all planets except Pluto and of the Jovian moons. Individual solar system objects are treated in the excellent series of books published by the University of Arizona Press: Faith Vilas, Clark R. Chapman, and Mildred Shapley Matthews (eds.), *Mercury* (1988); Richard P. Binzel, Tom Gehrels, and Mildred Shapley Matthews (eds.), *Asteroids II* (1989); Jay T. Bergstralh, Ellis D. Miner, and Mildred Shapley Matthews (eds.), *Uranus* (1991); Hugh H. Keiffer et al. (eds.), *Mars* (1992); Dale P. Cruikshank (ed.), *Neptune and Triton* (1995); S.W. Bougher, D.M. Hunten, and R.J. Phillips(eds.), *Venus II: Geology, Geophysics, Atmosphere, and Solar Wind Environment* (1997); and S. Alan Stern and David J. Tholen (eds.), *Pluto and Charon* (1997). Annually revised orbital and physical data about planets, moons, and selected comets and asteroids appear in *The Astronomical Almanac*, published by the U.S. Naval Observatory et al.; *The Observer's Handbook*, published annually by the Royal Astronomical Society of Canada, provides excellent information for observing solar system objects with the naked eye or small telescopes. International reports of research on asteroids, comets, meteorites, planets, moons, and other objects of the solar system appear regularly in *The Astrophysical Journal*, published by the American Astronomical Society and the University of Chicago; *The Astronomical Journal*, published by the

American Institute of Physics and the American Astronomical Society; *Astronomy and Astrophysics*, published by the European Southern Observatory; *Icarus*, a journal of solar system studies published by the American Astronomical Society's Division for Planetary Sciences; *Journal of Geophysical Research*, published by the American Geophysical Union; and *Annual Review of Earth and Planetary Sciences*. A superior monthly periodical for the nonprofessional, with regular coverage of the solar system and its constituents, is *Sky and Telescope*.

OUR SOLAR SYSTEM'S ORIGIN

An excellent collection of papers on the general subject of solar system origin appears in Vincent Mannings, Alan P. Boss, and Sara S. Russell (eds.), *Protostars & Planets IV* (2000); the volume includes papers about newly discovered planets around other stars. Volumes of original technical articles by different authors on facets of the topic are Richard Greenberg, André Brahic, and Mildred Shapley Matthews (eds.), *Planetary Rings* (1984); John F. Kerridge and Mildred Shapley Matthews (eds.), *Meteorites and the Early Solar System* (1988); and S.K. Atreya, J.B. Pollack, and Mildred Shapley Matthews (eds.), *Origin and Evolution of Planetary and Satellite Atmospheres* (1989). The origin and prevalence of ice in the solar system are treated at a popular level in Pat Dasch (ed.), *Icy Worlds of the Solar System* (2004). The formation of the inner planets has been extensively studied by George W. Wetherill, "Formation of the Earth," *Annual Review of Earth and Planetary Sciences*, 18:205–256 (1990), a review of his and others' work in the field.

INDEX

A

auroras, 66–68

B

Babcock, Harold, 14
Babcock, Horace, 14
Babcock magnetograph, 61
birefringent filter, 14

C

Callisto, 104
Cameron, Alistair G.W., 93
Carrington, Richard Christo-
    pher, 12
Cassini, Gian Domenico, 11
Centaur objects, 74, 77, 104
Ceres, 82, 11, 114, 115
Chamberlin, Thomas
    Chrowder, 92
Charon, 76, 77, 114
Chiron, 104
chromosphere, 15, 18, 19, 21,
    35–41, 48, 49, 56, 59, 60
corona, 10, 14, 15, 17, 18, 21,
    35–41, 44, 45, 48, 58, 59,
    61, 64, 86
coronagraph, 10, 14, 15, 17
coronal mass ejections, 17,
    46, 58, 68

coronal spectral lines, 13, 40

D

dwarf planets, 73, 77, 78, 80,
    82, 113–114

E

Earth, 6, 9, 10, 20, 21, 22, 25,
    26, 27, 28, 30, 40, 42, 43,
    44, 45, 53, 54, 56, 60, 61,
    64–69, 72, 77, 79, 80, 82,
    83, 84, 85, 86, 87, 89, 97,
    98, 101, 102, 103, 104,
    109, 110, 112, 113, 116
Edgeworth, Kenneth E., 74
emerging flux region (EFR),
    49, 50
Eris, 73, 76, 105, 114
European Space Agency, 18
Evershed effect, 48
exoplanets/ extrasolar plan-
    ets, 100–101, 109–110

F

51 Pegasi, 101, 110
Flamsteed, John, 10–11
flares, solar, 12, 16–17, 43, 46,
    58, 59–64, 68, 69, 85

Fraunhofer, Joseph von, 12, 19, 32, 33

G

Galilean satellites, 103
Galilei, Galileo, 10
Ganymede, 104
Grotrian, Walter, 13

H

Hale, George Ellery, 13, 14, 46
helioseismology, 28–30
Hodgson, R., 12

I

inner/ terrestrial planets, 79–82, 96–102
International Astronomical Union (IAU), 73, 82, 112, 113, 114
Io, 81

J

Jeans, James, 92
Jeffreys, Harold, 92
Jewitt, David, 75
Jupiter, 67–68, 72, 73, 77, 79–80, 81, 96, 98–99, 101, 104, 105, 107, 110, 113, 115

K

Kant, Immanuel, 89, 90, 91, 93, 96, 99, 108
Kirchhoff, Gustav R., 32
Kuiper belt, 73, 74–76, 77, 80, 81, 84, 99, 105, 111, 114

L

Laplace, Pierre-Simon, 90, 91, 93, 95, 99, 108
Leighton, Robert, 14
Little Ice Age, 54, 68
Luu, Jane, 75
Lyot, Bernard, 14

M

magnetograph, 61
magnetosphere, 65, 68, 80, 86
magnetotail, 65, 68
Mars, 72, 73, 79, 80, 99, 102, 104, 110, 113, 114
Maunder, E. Walter, 53
Maunder minimum, 54, 68
Mercury, 11, 72, 78, 79, 82, 102, 110, 113, 115, 116
Milky Way Galaxy, 19, 70, 92, 95
Moon, 20, 27, 35, 40, 71, 72, 80, 89, 98, 102, 104, 110
Moulton, Forest Ray, 92

N

Neptune, 44, 67, 72, 73, 74, 75, 76, 77, 80, 82, 84, 103, 105, 110, 111, 113, 114, 115
Newton, Isaac, 11, 89
Nicholson, Seth Barnes, 14

O

Oort cloud, 73, 75, 77, 79, 104–105
outer/ Jovian/ giant planets, 79–82, 102–104
 ring systems of, 105–108

P

Payne, Cecilia, 33
penumbra, 46, 48
photosphere, 15, 20, 21, 25, 27, 30, 31, 34, 35, 36, 38, 40, 41, 47, 48, 49, 56, 60
planetesimals/ planetary embryos, 102, 103, 105, 108
Pluto, 72, 73, 74, 76, 78, 79, 80, 105, 111, 113, 114
prominences, solar, 35, 38, 46, 56–59, 61
Proxima Centauri, 20
PSR B1257+12, 101, 109

R

Roche, Édouard, 105
Roche limit, 105, 107

S

Saturn, 43, 67, 72, 79, 80, 81, 98, 103, 105, 107, 110, 113
Scheiner, Christoph, 10
Schwabe, Samuel Heinrich, 11
Severny, A.B., 61
solar nebula, 6, 8, 91, 92, 94–96, 97, 98, 99, 103, 104, 108
solar oscillations, 14, 28, 29, 48
solar system
 angular momentum, 108
 asteroids and comets in, 82–85, 104–104
 composition of, 72–77
 early origin theories of, 90–93
 formation of, 6–8
 interplanetary medium of, 85–87
 modern origin theories of, 93–108
 orbits in, 77–79

planetary accretion, 96–104
planets and moons in,
79–82, 96–104, 105–108,
110–115
solar wind, 8, 17, 18, 19, 21,
26, 41–45, 54, 64, 65, 66,
67, 68, 85, 86, 87, 104,
108
spectroheliograph, 13, 14
spectroscopy, 12
Sun
atmosphere of, 27–41
formation of, 6-8
effect on earth, 64–69
evolution of, 25–27
history of the study of,
10–19
life span, 9
mass of, 6
specifications of, 19–22
structure of, 22–25
sunspots, 10, 11, 12, 13, 14,
18, 22, 25, 29, 30, 38, 40,
46, 47, 48, 49, 51, 53, 54,
55, 58, 59, 60, 63, 68
supernova, 19, 44, 87, 95

U

umbra, 46, 47, 48

Uranus, 67, 72, 79, 80, 105,
110

V

Venus, 9, 27, 72, 77, 79, 80,
102, 110, 113, 116

W

Wolf, Rudolf, 11–12

Y

Yerkes refractor, 13

Z

Zeeman effect, 13
Zurich relative sunspot number, 12